THE BOUNCE AND THE ECHO
Dying To Love A Game

D1715514

IAN JOHNSON

ATM Publishing • Brooklyn, NY
www.acrossthemargin.com

ISBN 978-0-9972417-4-7 (paperback)
ISBN 978-0-9972417-5-4 (e-book)
Library of Congress Control Number:
2019935713

To Dylan, Sila, Finley, and Mary,
and to the children of Siri Village.
May you all grow up wiser than your elders.

Contents

Part I: The Bounce

Part II: The Echo

Part I - The Bounce

Author's Note: Before I begin, let me state for the record that none of it was ever basketball's fault. It was just that, when things got bad, I didn't know who to blame, so I blamed the sport that was my life.

Chapter 1 — Indoctrination Part One

The French neighborhood of Montmartre in 1893 was to Paris what the East Village was to New York in the 1970s and 1980s, a hub of creativity and innovation. Moulin Rouge, with its distinctive red windmill, was four years old, attracting nightly visitors to the *Boulevard de Clichy*, from which those tourists could catch glimpses of the newfangled Eiffel Tower looming over the city to the southwest. France in the 1890s was in the midst of La Belle Époque, a forty-year period of unprecedented peace in Europe, of which Montmartre was perhaps the cultural capital. An all-star lineup of artists, from van Gogh to Renoir to Toulouse, populated Montmartre's smoky cafes, feeding off each other's creative energy, including that of Monet, who in 1893 was sketching for the first time the lily ponds that would become the subject of his most prominent work.

Additionally in Montmartre in 1893, just blocks from the blushing spectators ogling the cancan at Moulin Rouge, and perhaps within shouting distance of the silent brushstrokes coloring the canvases of some of art's greatest icons, was a YMCA in which the first basketball game on European soil was ever played. The organizer of the game was an American named Mel Rideout, a disciple of James Naismith, the PE instructor who two years earlier had invented basketball at another YMCA in Springfield, Massachusetts. Rideout was one of basketball's first missionaries, and over the next century the groundwork he laid spread across Europe, including to Spain, whose professional basketball league in 2006 counted among its members a team based out of Gijon, a city on the northern coast. Gijon's general manager, Raul, had just offered me a contract. Gijon didn't have the cultural cache of Paris in the 1890s, but its basketball courts were undoubtedly more modern.

My agent, a New Yorker named Mike Main, called me in Virginia with news of Gijon's offer. I had signed with Mike prior to graduating from Davidson College the previous spring. Over a breakfast of french toast at a cafe near campus, Mike had presented me with a binder in which he had organized, in color-coordinated sections, a hypothetical forecast of where and how my professional career might play out. The NBA was an unaddressed dream, too far off my horizon to consider, but the European leagues on the other hand were wide open. Mike showed me bios of his agency's contacts across the continent. Adrian in Spain. Miklos in Hungary. Pierre in France. I felt like I was being let in on a spy network, like I could point to a map and parachute down anywhere I wanted. When the waitress brought us the check, Mike signed the bill, and I signed with Mike.

I spent the summer after graduation at my parents' home in Virginia, waiting for the right offer from the right team. I was excited, yet unsure of what, exactly, I should be excited about. Europe was as abstract as college had become familiar, and accepting a new life in Europe would mean bidding goodbye to the one I'd leave behind. I wasn't sure I was ready. I had come into my own during my senior year, averaging career highs across the board and earning an abundance of postseason awards — All-Conference from both the media and coaches, NCAA Tournament Player of the Game, a square-inch portrait on the cover of *Sports Illustrated* — and cracking Davidson career lists in several statistical categories. I'd grown accustomed to my teammates' constant presence in my life, and now we'd live in different countries on different continents, never to be so proximate, so intimate, ever again.

The perks of a potential deal with Gijon, however, were pleasant distractions. The team played in an excellent league, and in addition to my tax-free monthly salary, they were going to lavish me with an apartment, a car, and a daily meal at a local restaurant. They'd also pay all my bills and toss in two round-trip flights. All I had to do was walk in the gym and ball out.

While Mike waited expectantly on the line from his office on Long Island, I talked out the situation with him, as if considering my options, feigning some autonomy in the matter. I'd had a number of other, mostly middling offers throughout the summer, from Sweden, Poland, and the Czech Republic, but turned them down in the same manner I considered the current one, on Mike's advice — he more or less dictated those nascent stages of my career.

Eventually I told Mike, as coolly as I could, that I accepted Gijon's offer. He said he'd get started on the paperwork and would call me in the morning. After hanging up the phone, I pulled out a world map and laid it across the kitchen table. I pinpointed Europe, zoomed in on Spain, and from four thousand miles away I looked down upon all the places I'd go.

In December 1891, a man named William R. Chase trudged through the snow to the International YMCA Training Center in Springfield, Massachusetts and arrived at the gym in time to hear his PE instructor, one Mr. Naismith (he hadn't yet earned his medical degree), outline a new activity. There'd been a lot of new activities lately at the YMCA, as Chase and his student peers were notoriously hard to keep engaged. Instructors came and went, as did their lesson plans, and there wasn't much initial enthusiasm for this new game Naismith was attempting to explain. Naismith pointed to peach baskets nailed to the overhang of the elevated running track and identified them as goals, then held up a soccer ball and said the object was to get the soccer ball in the goal. Pass the ball, no tackling, no dribbling. Nine players per team (a practical number, as there were only 18 students in the class). Chase distinguished himself that day by scoring the only bucket of the afternoon, the only point in the first game of basketball ever played. Others were less lucky, because despite Naismith's legislation against excessive physicality, some players somehow ended up with concussions, bruises, and bloody mouths. But the injuries were, in a way, a testament to the pleasure of Naismith's basket-ball, and before long it would be unusual *not* to see baskets hanging from the far ends of gymnasiums across the globe.

Exactly one hundred years later, in the winter of 1991, I was seven years old and playing organized competitive basketball for the first time in a local youth league in Pittsburgh, Pennsylvania. The focus of the game, my seven-year old brain was learning, wasn't to tap into a healthy competitive spirit — which was Naismith's original intention for the game — but rather to follow instructions. To this end coaches were gesticulating on the sidelines, yelling commands and inciting ideas of right and wrong. Everyone kept saying that all that mattered was that we did our best, but if the collective best of my team wasn't enough to win, then I was to feel disappointed. To reinforce this point, after losses the coaches would gather us in quiet corners of the gym to both solemnly list the reasons for our defeat and implore us to think about what we could do better next time. The enduring message was that only when our team scored more points than the other team was anyone allowed to feel content with themselves. Unlike William Chase and his fellow students, I didn't go home after my games concussed or bloodied, but I was indoctrinated all the same, having understood a very important truth about sports in America — that sports are a lot more than the happy virtuous thing we claim them to be.

Not long after that first youth season ended, my family — my parents, two sisters and me — left Pittsburgh and followed my dad's new job down to Charlottesville, Virginia. The first time I climbed the stairs in our new house — I was nine years old — I noticed a large dead insect on the second step up from the landing. This was ominous and somehow dangerous, I intuited, and from that day forward I didn't set foot on that step again, not even when helping carry heavy furniture, for fear of the supposed horrible events that contact with that step would set in motion.

In avoiding the insect I had succumbed, it seemed, to some innate instinct that associated seemingly random occurrences with vague but substantial fears. More fears quickly followed. I started collecting basketball cards, and to complement my collection I bought a series of *Beckett* magazines that informed me, say, that my 1991 *Upper Deck* Vinny Del Negro card was worth thirty-seven cents. I would often read the magazines before bed, and in doing so, I somehow developed elaborate *Beckett*-related bedtime routines, which involved flipping through a sequence of "correct" pages a "correct" number of times, a mandatory procedure that I had to fulfill before I could allow myself to fall asleep. If the process felt funny, I'd have to repeat it, sometimes waiting another hour or more before the time felt right again. I was never certain what would happen if I didn't flip through *Beckett* in the "correct" way, at the "correct" time, but I didn't want to find out. Every now and then I'd try to circumvent the routine and defiantly throw myself under the covers, but no matter how tired I was I could never let it go, and the magazine would always come out, the routine reprocessed.

Eventually these strange symptoms broke free of the privacy of home. I played in tournaments in middle school where, during timeouts, I performed elaborate rituals with my fingers, making Spock-like motions and/or using my thumb to touch each of my fingertips in succession, a certain number of times, while the coaches jabbered about strategy and implored me to grab more rebounds. Not performing these finger rituals, I reasoned, would translate into poor play on the court, or, worse, into something more horrific, like an injury to my mother or perhaps even death.

These symptoms grew to become a significant part of my life, but they were never overly debilitating and they were never something I couldn't hide, and so, not knowing any different, I assumed they were a normal part of being a kid. I didn't yet know the words "obsessive" and "compulsive," and I certainly didn't know the word "disorder." The overt

6

narrative of my life, reinforced by everyone in it, was that everything was perfectly okay. And if everything was perfectly okay, how could anything be wrong? Like many boys, I had learned from a young age that males should be steely and cold-blooded, that we shouldn't cry and should never admit weakness. Even before a long line of coaches reinforced this narrative, I knew it by heart.

There was nothing wrong, for instance, the night I snuck down into the basement where my older sister, Hannah, had a few friends over. I found Hannah curled up under a blanket, asleep, but when I shook her she didn't move. I shook her harder but she was still motionless. I slapped her face several times and got the same result. I didn't know a thing about the effects of alcohol, much less that my thirteen-year-old big sister was drinking it regularly in large quantities. In a panic, I shook her harder for what seemed like minutes. "Go away, Ian," she managed to get out when her eyes finally fluttered open, and so I did, shoving the memory deep into my core.

There was nothing wrong either when, after I obtained my driver's license, I drove the winding and sloping back roads near my house at night, one hand on the wheel, the other on the headlights, daring myself to switch them off for seconds at a time. I imagined swerving into oncoming traffic, sometimes getting really scared that I might actually do it, scared enough for me to have to grip both hands on the steering wheel and concentrate really hard on staying between the lines.

There was still nothing wrong when, still in high school, I copied a poem about suicide into my journal, glad that I'd found a piece of literature with which I could relate. I was so proud of this that I showed the poem to my mom, who understandably panicked and begged me to tell her if anything was wrong. "No, mom, I'm fine," I assured her, and made up some excuse as to why I had copied it.

Before I became really good at basketball, I was skinny and had braces and wore clunky glasses. I played the flattering loyal pet with the girls at school, thinking I could never get their attention otherwise. I was somewhat absent-minded — the kind of kid you'd see slack-jawed, staring off into the distance — and was bullied by the kids in my neighborhood because in me they sensed a victim who was too scared to fight back. Sometimes they would pelt my ribs with their fists until I couldn't breathe, or would hold me against a tree and take turns blowing smoke in my face. Worse was when they'd get going verbally, just to see if I would break, but fortunately by then I was good at hiding my pain, including from myself, and I never broke. When the neighborhood kids weren't being bullies they were the guys I sometimes had fun with, which I think made the situation worse, never knowing which version of them I was going to get.

I wanted to change but I didn't know how. My sister Hannah was popular at school, and she told me once that if I got contacts, dressed better, and hung out with different people that I might one day be cool, too. My teenage wardrobe selections were debatable, but I did get taller and started scoring more points on the court, and suddenly things changed all on their own. I still had braces and glasses, was still what pop culture would call an airhead or a dork, but the only people who made fun of me anymore were my teammates, in a brotherly kind of way. The bullies in my neighborhood stopped punching me for no reason, and the kids at school began to seek out *my* approval of *them*, as if I was suddenly some bestower of coolness. All because I had begun to show them that I could play ball.

The trouble was, I'd only gotten better at basketball, and hadn't grown by a corresponding degree as a human being. It was therefore challenging to accept the new dynamics that basketball was affording me. But as long as I was good at basketball, I learned I'd be okay, and so I quietly vowed to keep getting better.

As much as I loved the game in its raw form, I began to see formal basketball (AAU, high school, anything involving adults) as a kind of social forgery, a system that couldn't be as great as everyone claimed if it promoted confused fakers like me. I figured that if formal basketball was truly legitimate, its adult practitioners would notice how troubled I was and either kick me out or demand I change. If anyone noticed me beneath the surface, they didn't say so. This was somewhat disconcerting, but faking my way up through the system was far, far better than being my scared self outside of it, and so in the system I stayed.

I continued to grow up in the system, quite literally. One spring I grew four inches and gained thirty pounds in about three months, a growth spurt that troubled my balance and kept my knees and Achilles in constant rebellion. I sometimes spontaneously fell, prompting more coordinated teammates to jovially cry out, "Timber!" when I hit the deck. At a game in Roanoke, Virginia the crowd chanted, "Go, Go, Gadget!" whenever I shot free throws, in reference to my gangly limbs.

My talent seemed to increase proportionally to my height, and the adults in my life soon began to whisper of a career that stretched far beyond anything my adolescent brain could imagine. If I hadn't already, I began to associate success with some fugue idea of "making it." In other words, I stopped playing for fun and instead began to chase the future. The better I played, the more inescapable the future became. Several years later, in Spain, that future finally arrived.

When Ernest Hemingway arrived in Spain in 1937, he was on assignment for the American newspaper *Alliance,* covering the Spanish Civil War. His colleague at the time was Martha Gellhorn, a fellow journalist covering the war for *Collier's Weekly*. Hemingway married Gellhorn in 1940, the same year his novel *For Whom the Bell Tolls* was published, based on his experiences enmeshed with anti-Franco Republican forces outside of Madrid. In just a couple of years on Spanish soil, Hemingway secured himself a dynamic wife, wrote a timeless novel, and still found time to fight the fascist bad guys as part of a rebel army. My own plans for my new career in Spain were just as lofty.

After getting off the phone with Mike, I stared at my world map for a long time. Each country on the map was a different color. Spain was an alluring shade of orange, the color of a basketball. As I set my finger down and practiced the city's pronunciation (*Hghee-hon*), I quickly constructed the entirety of my professional career, fantasizing in sweeping arcs how I would live out the next five to ten years. I would dominate the Spanish league, colonize Spanish women, and master the Spanish language. When Mike faxed me the multilingual contract the next day, it felt like he was late to the party, as Spain, in my head, was already happening.

A few weeks later I sat folded into economy class on an Iberia Airlines 777 as the aircraft jumped up off the sweltering August tarmac at Dulles International Airport in Virginia and ascended into the unfolding twilight. Below, the darkening Atlantic Ocean looked like a million pairs of blue jeans stretching towards Europe, towards Spain, and towards Gijon. When we landed, it would not be on a map.

Because of my height, I was allowed a seat in front of the bulkhead, directly across from the little flip-down bench where the flight attendant buckles in for takeoffs and landings. This particular flight attendant was female, petite, and pretty. She and I chatted amicably in Spanish for segments of the flight, and by the time she served me my meal I was pretty sure that I was in love. I waited for her to tell me she lived in Gijon. I imagined our future together. We'd date. She'd come to my games. Maybe we'd get married.

As the plane touched down in Madrid, with the passengers standing and stretching once we hit the gate ready to shuffle onto the jetway, I noticed the flight attendant yawning. We'd stopped talking by then (we hadn't talked much at all, actually, at least not outside of my head; flight attendants, apparently, can be busy people), and to revive the conversation, after catching her yawn a second time, I planned to ask her if she was tired (stimulating, I know). But, tired myself, I mixed up a few Spanish phrases, and so my last words to her, spoken hand-over-mouth to mask my morning breath, were "Are you sad?" Her expression briefly revealed the extent of her exhaustion but she didn't otherwise respond.

I cruised towards customs with a little bounce in my step. My European adventure was off to a solid start: an entire romantic relationship had already unfolded, and I still had a connecting flight.

In 1965, the Italian Lega Basket Serie A, in hopes of raising its flagging standard of play, decided to allow its member clubs to sign one foreigner each. The 1965-66 season saw the league's twelve teams sign eleven Americans and one Yugoslavian, the most notable foreigner being Bill Bradley, a Princeton All-American and beloved collegiate icon. Bradley, selected as a territorial pick by New York in the '65 NBA draft, turned down the Knicks after college and chose instead to attend Oxford on a Rhodes scholarship. In between P.P.E. (Politics, Philosophy, and Economics) classes he commuted to Italy once a week as the sole permitted foreign player for Simmenthal, a team based in Milan.

Bradley and his cohorts established European norms for American players that still largely existed in 2006. Foreign players had their taxes paid by the team, were provided with apartments, transportation, and food, and in return the "import" players were expected to lead the team to a championship. In the spring of '66 Bradley did just that, leading Simmenthal to the European title, the first for an Italian club, with a 77-72 win over CSKA Moscow.

Forty years later, my tacit agreement with Gijon was to accomplish more or less the same. On a Saturday night two weeks into my tenure, the players and their wives and girlfriends (if we had them) gathered at a swank restaurant a couple blocks from the Bay of Biscay for a group dinner. It was almost midnight by the time the tapas were brought out — thinly sliced cod, olives stuffed with red peppers, and a buttery shrimp scampi. To drink, we shared bottles of a hard cider native to northern Spain, sidra, which is traditionally poured like this: The pourer holds the bottle high above the head, as if trying to water ceiling plants, and the receiving glass low by one's waist, as if begging for loose change. With a wingspan's distance between bottle and glass, the pourer attempts to direct an ounce or so of the cider into the cup, at which point the uber-effervescent bubbly is quickly downed by the drinker before the bubbles dissipate.

I sat near a teammate named Jesus (pronounced *Hay-zeus*), who handed me a bottle and a glass and suggested I attempt the traditional pour. It was easier than it sounds, and when I'd filled up two cups Jesus and I toasted and dug into a plate of shrimp. Everyone was uncorking and unwinding (it was our first day off during the preseason), and amidst the din of imbibement Jesus leaned over and asked me, softly, "You've been here a couple of weeks now. What do you think?"

"About the team?"

"Yeah, your experience so far."

I popped a shrimp into my mouth and chewed slowly, stalling as I considered the data points up to then. It was a good question. What *did* I think?

There was nobody at the airport to pick me up when my connecting flight landed. The regional airport that serves Gijon isn't very large, and the baggage claim area is especially small. With my brand new L.L. Bean suitcase stacked on my stuffed Davidson gym bag, I stood as erect as possible near the whispering sliding doors, hoping for a look of recognition in the eyes of someone I did not yet know.

"Somebody will be there to pick you up when you land," Mike had told me.

As late morning shifted into early afternoon, it was hard not to panic. Whenever those sliding doors opened and someone walked in or out, I could see Spain, but Spain, apparently, was not ready for me, at least not without an escort. I had to use the restroom but steadfastly refused to go, fearing the moment I went would be the exact moment my ride showed up. Eventually the team's GM, Raul, middle-aged with thick brown hair and trailing a whiff of woody cologne, showed up, full of "Ha, ha, sorry-I'm-two-hours-late" grins. I told him it was no big deal, and to offset any guilt he might have felt, I profusely thanked him for coming all the way to get me.

On our way into Gijon, Raul dished about the team and the city. I wanted to appear excited and interested, but all hands were on deck just to keep me awake. At one point I fell asleep to the lispy drone of his voice, waking up an indeterminable spell later to the same ongoing drone.

Our first stop was the arena. We parked on a curb fifty or so yards away from some windowless back entrance, through which a small, boyish-looking man emerged. Raul and I stepped out to greet him.

"The assistant coach," Raul said with a hint of reverence, as if we were celebrity-spotting. "Marcos."

Marcos approached but stopped some ten feet away from the car, looking at me cautiously, as if I might at any second challenge him to a duel. He pulled out a pack of cigarettes, extracted one, and set it between his lips. His lighter flicked, flicked again, and then finally caught, Marcos squinting at me over the flame. He took a long drag before addressing Raul. They spoke too fast for me to keep up, but I caught a thread and soon it was clear Topic

14

1A was yours truly. Marcos kept his gaze trained in my direction like I might run away, his eyes running up and down my body. I was trying to stand straighter and look tougher, while simultaneously trying to ignore the urge to walk up to Marcos and punch him in the face. A minute later Marcos stabbed the butt of his cigarette into the concrete, nodded at Raul, and retreated back into the arena.

Raul and I got back into the car and drove to my new residence, a multi-story brick building on a claustrophobic city street. My second-floor apartment opened onto a long corridor with rooms spaced like offices down each side, each of which was empty. There was no furniture. The walls were bare and the windows devoid even of curtains, save for one room at the end in which lay a double bed wrapped in wrinkled, faintly odorous mismatched sheets (one of my Spanish teammates and his wife, I would learn, shared the bed for weeks prior to my arrival). I considered asking Raul for a fresh set, but didn't want to seem incommodious.

As if to distract me from the bedroom, Raul led me back down to the kitchen, which was, like every other room in the place, bare and empty. There was a refrigerator and a microwave, but no cutlery or dishes, no table or chairs, no pots or pans. He showed me a television in one of the side rooms, the kind with wooden trim around the screen and a dial to manually change the channel, but there was no couch or chair on which to sit and watch. Down the hall, Raul flipped on the light in the bathroom. The sink was crusty, the mirror smudged. There was no shower curtain, and the toilet seat was some kind of flimsy plastic.

"This place is just temporary," Raul said, as if reading my

mind. "Give us a week or so and you'll be in your new flat."

"No, it's okay," I replied with enthusiasm, as if I'd lived in the woods my whole life. "Esta bien."

To assuage any guilt Raul might have had at putting me up in such a run down place, I thanked him enthusiastically for setting it up. Raul seemed skeptical of my gratitude, and then, as if to remind me what I was here to do, told me some guy named Jesus would pick me up soon for practice.

An hour later, Jesus and I were bumping and honking our way through late afternoon congestion. Like most European cities, Gijon's roads weren't laid out with vehicular mass commuting in mind, and as the minutes ticked away the prospect of being late for my first practice was enough to boil up something serious in my gut. Jesus, however, was friendly and wanted to speak English, and for a few minutes I almost didn't feel alone. I listened intently as he told me about the team, not because I was all that curious but because I hoped somewhere in there he'd say something like, *Don't worry, it'll all be okay.*

The first drill in practice was a standard layup shuffle. I gripped the ball, took a couple of dribbles towards the hoop, and laid it up off the backboard. Most likely the first shot I ever made was a layup, back in that youth league in Pittsburgh, and I'd made hundreds of thousands since. Layups were familiar and reflexive, and as I loosened up my fatigue and nerves lifted and faded.

But, like any drug, the high wanes, and as my teammates and I set off on more complicated drills, ones that required focus, I slouched and drooped, feeling somehow both cooperative and encumbering at the same time.

After practice, Raul dropped me back off at my apartment. Before he left, I asked him where I could get some dinner. He pointed vaguely in a few different directions, then nodded rapidly with wide eyes as if to say, *Good enough?* I looked at him blankly, then nodded back. He gave a final nod and told me he had somewhere to be, then shooed me out of his car and sped away.

As the Iberian sun sank over the skyline, I wandered in search of sustenance, passing a few restaurants whose menus were propped on lecterns on the sidewalk, but for some reason I didn't venture inside. Eventually, I found a fast-food-ish joint where I ordered a trove of chicken sandwiches, quickly devoured them, then ordered a few more for breakfast. On the way out, I grabbed handfuls of plastic silverware from the little bins by the ketchup dispenser, which would serve as my utensils for the next month.

Exiting the restaurant, and desperate to get back home and climb into bed, I realized I'd been so intent on finding food that I'd neglected to pay attention to the route I'd taken from my apartment. I clenched my to-go bag, the heat of the sandwiches warming my fingers through the thin paper, the pilfered silverware bulging my pockets, and started walking, more lost with each step, panic humming in my toes, and suppressing urges to cry and/or scream. My first day in Spain had gone utterly mierda.

Standing on the curb that night — any curb, I stood on many — sucking in exhaust under muted European street lights, crashing after a meal of fried chicken sandwiches, and fatigued to heights I hadn't known existed, I'm not sure I'd ever felt so alone, before or since.

When I did finally make it back to my apartment, I had to endure a rush of novel obsessive-compulsive symptoms that kept me up long into what should've been a good night's sleep. I stood on one foot in the doorway to the bedroom, flipping the light on and off a specific number of times, over and over again, until it felt "right." I rolled over in bed a certain number of times, then got out of bed and went back to the lightswitch, where I repeated the process, again and again.

In the summer of 1995, Dominique Wilkins, the Human Highlight Film, future NBA Hall-of-Famer and eventual 13th highest scorer on the NBA's career list, was upset. The Atlanta Hawks, with whom he'd earned 9 All-Star bids and 7 All-NBA selections (but no NBA championship), had traded him a year earlier to the NBA's perennial cellar dweller Los Angeles Clippers, and the following season, in which he'd signed as a free agent with the Boston Celtics, saw his scoring average dip to a career low. Instead of trying to find another NBA team for the 1995-96 season, Wilkins chose instead to play for the Greek club Panathinaikos BSA Athens, following in the footsteps of fellow NBA legends Bob McAdoo, Darryl Dawkins, and George Gervin (among others), each of whom had spent time luxuriating in the sunny Mediterranean air following their NBA careers — European stints that were largely seen as celebratory, career-capping curtain calls.

In 1995, when Wilkins landed in Athens to thousands of screaming fans and a police escort to his new digs, American imports were still dominating the European basketball landscape, but they were no longer novelties and were no longer godly. Despite global domination by the United States Dream Team in 1992, by Dream Team II at the World Championships in Toronto in '94 (for whom Wilkins played), and by the third Dream Team iteration at the '96 Olympics in Atlanta, Georgia, Europeans were closing the gap. The U.S. margin of victory was dropping steadily in every international competition (a trend that would continue until 2006, when Jerry Colangelo and Mike Krzyzewski decided enough was enough), and trailblazers like Croatian Drazen Petrovic and Lithuanian Arvydas Sabonis were establishing a foothold for Europeans in the NBA.

Across the Atlantic, top European teams entered a kind of flux where they were eager to utilize American talent while at the same time trying to prove to the U.S. that European clubs could hang without American help. It was into this dynamic that Wilkins waded when he arrived in Greece, where despite earning $3.5 million in tax-free salary and living in a four-story marbled villa with a maid and a chauffeur, he had some trouble getting comfortable. He was easily the best player on his team (and perhaps in all of Europe), satisfyingly led Panathinaikos to the 1996 European championship, and earned MVP honors at the Final Four in Paris. However, his discipline-minded coach never fully embraced him, trying for much of the season to get him to play in a style not suited to Wilkins' game. "I reached my frustration point," Wilkins told a reporter near the end of his first season, describing a complaint-airing encounter with team management, "I said, I'm tired of being treated like crap, I'm not going to be treated like that anymore." For his efforts, Wilkins was fined $40,000, and soon after rumors surfaced that Wilkins was trying to buy out his own contract.

By 2006, just a decade later, international players had thoroughly infiltrated the NBA, with 83 non-American players from 37 countries suiting up for 28 of the league's 30 teams, including future all-time legends Manu Ginobili (Argentina), Dirk Nowitzki (Germany), and Spain's own Pau Gasol. Four years earlier, the American grip on global basketball dominance had been shaken with a horrifying 6th place finish at the 2002 World Championships in Indianapolis, Indiana where a shell-shocked U.S. team lost for the first time since the the International Basketball Federation (FIBA) and the NBA allowed NBA players to participate in international competition, a streak of 58 games dating back to 1992. Ginobili's Argentina and Gasol's Spain both edged the U.S. in a tournament that saw Nowitzki named MVP and the Americans finish behind New Zealand.

Perhaps the most apt comparison to the U.S. debacle in Indiana is a wine-tasting held in Paris in 1976, which saw a panel of European judges — a who's who of the best French sommeliers and vitners — blindly rank a '73 Californian Cabernet Sauvignon and a '73 Napa Valley Chardonnay higher than any of the contest's respective French reds and whites. Going in, the competition was seen as a foregone conclusion, with only one journalist bothering to cover the event, and then only as a favor to a friend.

When one of the French judges heard the results, she demanded her ballot back and complained that the evaluative criteria were faulty. French papers ignored or refused to cover the event, sore-loser sentiments that were echoed in the aftermath of U.S. basketball losses in 2002, when proud and angry American basketball nationalists ticked off a list of excuses to explain their 6th place finish on the court, refusing to accept that the international game had evolved to a point where teams could do more than just throw rocks at the throne.

Known today as the "Judgement in Paris," the 1976 wine tasting was regarded as proof that American winemakers had taken a European tradition and made it their own. "It was the most important event," the lone journalist at the event, *Time* magazine's George Taber, told NPR on the event's 40th anniversary in 2016, "because it broke the myth that only in France could you make great wine. It opened the door for this phenomenon today of the globalization of wine."

In 1978, the same ten or so wines from two years earlier were re-tested, again blindly, on the assumption that French wines would age better than their American counterparts. But this time the American wines scored even higher, to the continued bafflement and chagrin of the French. In 2004, after two years of soul-searching, Team USA basketball similarly once again took to the floor in international competition, this time at the Olympics in Athens, Greece, hoping to avenge and reestablish with a gold medal what the 2002 squad had squandered in Indianapolis. But, just like the French winemakers, the U.S. team got punched on the other cheek, getting blown out by Puerto Rico in the preliminary round and losing to Argentina in the semifinals before salvaging a bronze medal against Lithuania. 2002 was no fluke. The American myth was broken.

American players in Europe in 2006, then, lacked the mystique they once had, and therefore had a little more to prove, but there were encouraging signs my first couple of weeks in Gijon. I was finally shown the restaurant where I could procure my daily meal, and I found a small grocery store not far from my apartment where I bought yogurts for breakfast and boxes of muesli to snack on. I conducted a flawless introductory press conference, where I said all the right things, impressing the media with my Spanish 301, and I found an internet cafe where I could check in on happenings back home. Jesus and I became friends, chatting for a few minutes each day before practice. He was curious about America, and I about his country.

And then there was basketball.

Gijon's head coach, Diego, was a super-thin man with extra-long limbs and an unfortunate gait that earned him the nickname El Pinguino. When I met him, he was in the first weeks of his first year as a head coach, still feeling the position out. Diego was hard to get a read on, in that he was, for lack of a more sensitive term, somewhat bipolar in his moods. He'd huddle us up to introduce a drill, grinning like he'd just invented the three-man weave, jabbing his foot and flapping his arms seal-like while he talked, and then he would step back and implore us to execute. Invariably, for one or many of a multitude of reasons, we would mess up the drill, and when we did Diego would swiftly waddle out onto the court and flash us his empty palms, fingers pointed down like the bankrupt guy on Monopoly's Community Chest card, whining away. Then, later in practice we would do another drill, or maybe the very same drill in the very same way, and he'd praise us like we were the Dream Team. His outbursts, of either anger or acclaim, were random, and our performances in the drills that preceded them of no seeming influence. Or so I say because, as a team, we were pretty consistently lackadaisical.

It's hard to blame Diego for his mood swings. He was newly hired and coaching at a level where even successful, seasoned coaches often sit squarely on the chopping block. In this anxiety-simmering, what-have you-won-for-me-lately atmosphere, every drill, every shot, every dribble, by any player at any time, is a reflection of how well the coach is imparting his authority. Or a commentary on how some coaches, particularly first-year coaches, perceive things to be, especially when GMs and team presidents watch practice from the sidelines, arms crossed and stone faced.

Even if I didn't blame Diego, I don't think I ever respected him. I don't know if any of us did. I remember a day early on in the season in which the drill called for us to bank in three three-pointers in a row. Twelve guys were running around trying to bank in threes, but there were only two baskets and everyone was shooting at the same time and our balls were hitting each other and flying all over the place. A lot of us were having trouble just banking in one basket, let alone three in a row, and then the situation became humorous because, come on, they were *paying* us to do this kind of stuff. Soon guys were laughing and grinning and Diego couldn't tell us to stop because it was his baby of a drill, and so he started yelling at us from the sideline and the more red-faced he became the more amused we all were.

At the end of practice Diego would gather us at mid-court. He would look around and squint, eyes darting this way and that, as if someone was about to shoot him with a water gun, and then, some indeterminate number of seconds later, he'd raise an arm, drop it like a gavel, and with quivering lips say "Suficiente."

I never respected Diego, as I didn't believe he ever deserved to be. But the counter to that is, should he have respected *me*? For the first time in my life, after fifteen years of school teams and AAU, of driveway workouts and road trips to podunk backwoods cities, I was getting paid to play ball. Paid to make layups and jump shots and jump hooks. Paid to body my man on defense. Paid to play a *game*. It was a confusing feeling, as I didn't necessarily feel like an asset worth financial compensation.

I certainly worked hard, and I hustled in practice, and never missed a session in the weight room. I generally knew how to execute our plays (as well as anyone on the team), was always punctual, gave high-fives, and didn't do anything to sully my reputation.

I worked hard mentally, too, but the hard work I did in my head mostly took the form of sharpening and rehearsing my internal monologues, the ones in which I sandblasted Diego for all the crappy qualities he exhibited as a coach. I searched for his faults like loose change under car seats, and when I identified one I caricatured him for it, delivering harsh verdicts in long or short-winded speeches conducted under my breath. That nobody else seemed to like him either made things easier, and when other guys on the team made fun of Diego, I felt good and made sure I laughed and did what I could to encourage more.

One day at practice I missed a rotation on defense, at which point Diego stopped the scrimmage to let me know.

"Okay, but," I protested, "but there should've been..." I trailed off.

Normally quick to launch into words himself, this time Diego instead stayed quiet.

"Que? What, Ian? Tell me."

Everyone in the gym fell silent, as coach-player conflicts are often wildly entertaining.

"No, nevermind," I said, waving him off, as if he wouldn't understand anyway.

"No. Tell me. What happened?"

What had happened was I'd missed a rotation, but because my most intangible of intangibles, my attitude, had been compromised by fear and uncertainty, I couldn't admit it, not even to myself, and so I blamed the easiest target, Diego.

 The best part of my day was the few minutes of euphoric relief I received after our evening practice finished. It was nice when morning practices wrapped up, but nice in the way you feel when you finish mowing the front yard, yet knowing you still have to do the back. I could relax somewhat in the evenings, and it was in these brief windows of darkness, where, despite the onslaught of obsessive-compulsive symptoms, I could convince myself that moving to Europe to play basketball was worth it.

The most accurate and honest assessment of my first weeks in Spain was this: I hated nearly *everything*. Gijon was unfamiliar and power-driven, the situation both more and less challenging than I'd expected, and my mind was having trouble adapting. Part of the problem was that the real Gijon clashed violently with the Gijon I'd imagined back in Virginia when I'd placed my finger on my map and dreamed. It was expectation versus reality, and I desperately wanted things to be better than they seemed. *How was Spain not the proverbial dream?* Even if I wasn't in the NBA, I was still a professional basketball player, the kind of thing kids stood up in third grade to formally declare as their life's intention. The kind of thing schoolteachers and parents shrugged off with amused grins. I'd wished for this as a ten-year-old myself, and there I was, wish fulfilled.

On the phone and in emails to family and friends back home, I couldn't say Spain was anything but great. I couldn't say Spain wasn't anything but everything I'd wanted it to be, because I thought saying so would reflect poorly on me, and therein was my dilemma: I could not separate the situation I was in from myself in the situation. I had to convince myself that everything was okay, so I could be okay. I had to lie, and I would. I'd lie to myself and to my friends, to my family and to the organization, and, at a team dinner at an oceanside restaurant two weeks into my first season, to Jesus.

What did I think so far?

"I love it," I told Jesus, reaching for another shrimp and ignoring his unconvinced look, instead directing my attention back towards the table at large, where talk had turned to relationships.

"I could never have an athlete as a girlfriend," someone said.

"Really?" someone else eagerly chimed in. "I can only date athletes. They understand."

With semi-seriousness, the table debated the pros and cons of dating athletes and non-athletes alike.

"And you, Ian, how do you like your women?"

The table quieted, eyes converging.

I wasn't expecting the sudden rush of attention. It felt like a test, that there was a right answer. My teammates waited expectantly, and the wives and girlfriends, too polite to stare, eyed me furtively behind their Malbecs.

My lips twitched. *How did I like my women?*

"Desnuda?" I said, with a shrug. "Naked?"

There was laughter, and the conversation pivoted away from me, and I turned back to Jesus. "Yeah man, I love it here," I told him again.

Jesus studied me for a moment, lifted one of his shoulders to his cheek in rightful European skepticism, held it there for a second, then let it drop.

"We'll see," he said.

Chapter 2 — Indoctrination Part Two

In 1969, NBC paid $500,000 to become the first major network to broadcast the championship game of the NCAA Men's Basketball Tournament, treating a national audience to a 37-point gem from UCLA's Lew Alcindor as he helped secure the third of seven straight titles for his legendary coach, John Wooden.

Thirty years earlier, in 1940, NBC's flagship station in New York, W2XBS, aired an afternoon doubleheader at Madison Square Garden, the first ever basketball games to be transmitted via cathode ray. It's estimated that fewer than 400 New York households had televisions at the time (a top of the line set in 1940 could ring up as high as $600, about $10,000 in 2016 dollars), but nonetheless, televised college basketball was officially switched on.

By 2002, there were far more than 400 television sets in America, and on November 22nd of that year a good number of them were tuned to ESPN to watch powerhouse Duke, the Goliath, take on my new team Davidson, the David, in our first game of the year.

Warming up, I heard someone in Duke's student section shouting some very intimate things he was planning on doing to my sisters, commentary both detailed and personal. I scanned the stands until I spotted amid the sea of blue a guy I knew from home, a guy I was sure I'd been friends with in high school. We locked eyes. He glared. I frowned.

"This is it," one of our assistants confirmed in the locker room a few minutes before tip-off. "It's real now."

I started the game on the bench, hands gripping a damp towel, not bothering to think when, or if, I would get to play. I just hoped it looked like I belonged, and that my friends and family back home would catch glimpses of me on television. But when one of our starting big men was whistled for his second foul just a few minutes into the game, Coach spun towards me and pointed. I stood up, tossed my towel aside and ripped off my warmup. I strode to the scorer's table and checked into the game, into the blank canvas of my college career, momentarily forgetting everything that had led up to that moment.

In the spring following my junior season of high school, I tried out for and was offered a spot on the team at Oak Hill Academy, the famed basketball powerhouse in Mouth of Wilson, Virginia. The previous year, Oak Hill had enjoyed an undefeated season en route to a mythical national championship, the school's fourth. That June, one of their players, Desagana Diop, would be selected 8th by the Dallas Mavericks in the NBA Draft. Perhaps a little inflated by the idea of connoting my name with the school, I accepted the coach's offer, which meant I would leave home for my senior year.

Back home in Charlottesville following my tryout, I went to get shots up at my soon-to-be-former high school gym, but when I went to retrieve the two balls I typically used, they weren't in their normal spot.

My soon-to-be-former high school coach suddenly

appeared, as if he'd been waiting for me. I'd told him the news earlier that morning. "Basketballs are for current players only," he told me, red-faced.

A little later that summer, still in Charlottesville, I was at school for a group workout when someone from the athletic office approached and told me to check the trash can by my former coach's desk. "Door's open," he said.

During a water break I entered the office, and inside the trash can, next to a candy wrapper and a damp tea bag, was a stack of recruiting letters, all addressed to me via the school, including letters from top-tier programs like North Carolina. My ex-coach had been throwing them away. Plenty of other letters, however, did make it into my mailbox, and my recruitment intensified. In August 2001, months before I needed to make any kind of final commitment, I departed for Oak Hill to spend my senior year.

The Oak Hill campus is nestled in the hills of Appalachia, a part of the world blessed with four seasons, full sunsets, and fiery leaves committing gentle suicide in fall before blossoming green again in spring. The Oak Hill Warriors gym is cramped, with barely enough room for a full court and five rows of bleachers on one side. On the baseline wall hang the jerseys of Oak Hill alumni who have gone on to become collegiate All-Americans, and on the other end hang banners denoting Oak Hill's national championships and top five finishes. There is barely enough room for these either.

When classes started that fall, I was still processing the idea of being a student at a boarding school in the woods, an idea that was previously reserved for young adult novels. But I quickly got used to Oak Hill's quirks and rhythms. There was an imaginary line down the center of campus which divided the boys and girls' dorms. Get caught on the wrong side and face immediate expulsion, or so went the threat, but, if you managed to sneak across the line for a covert rendezvous, you reaped a blitz of adolescent thrill. I didn't smoke, but cigarettes sometimes traded for $20 a pop, depending on demand, with cigarettes just one item in a black market of contraband whose stock was smuggled onto campus with Cold War-worthy concealment tactics.

At Oak Hill, practice was practice, except that our practices were with guys a little taller and more talented than any other high school practice in America. We had nine players who would go on to play Division I basketball, and one of my new teammates, a guy from Baltimore, Maryland named Carmelo Anthony, was supposedly one of the two top high school players in the country, his competition a kid from Akron, Ohio named LeBron James. LeBron at the time wore Adidas, but our locker room was stocked with Jordan gear, as we were one of the few high schools in America to be sponsored by His Airness.

My college recruitment was ongoing at Oak Hill. Not being particularly people-smart, it was nearly impossible for me to tell the difference between one recruiting pitch and another, whether it was better to be a Wildcat or a Hokie or a Crimson. But I liked everything I'd seen and heard about Davidson College, and one morning in September I walked into Coach Steve Smith's office having made up my mind.

"I'm ready to commit to Davidson," I told him.

"You sure about this?" Coach asked.

I wasn't sure, but nor was I not sure. My commitment was just something that was going to happen, and Davidson seemed like a great place, and Coach Bob McKillop, a great coach.

I called the Davidson coaching staff and told them the news, and then after leaving Coach Smith's office I sauntered off to study period in the library, where somebody had turned on the television in time to learn that a plane had crashed into one of the World Trade Center towers in New York City. There was no class that afternoon, only a schoolwide assembly where the school's president told us that our lives had changed forever that day.

On a roster with nine future Division I players, I wasn't particularly needed at Oak Hill, and I spent a lot of the season confused by the spectacle of top-level high school ball. People lined up for my autograph after games in which I didn't score. I was a really good high school player, but I harbored no illusions, even back then, that so much of sports was built on *myth*, that the jersey I wore was paramount to the human on whose shoulders it hung.

After a game somewhere in North Carolina, I approached a female fan outside the arena, got her number, then called her a few days later from the communal dorm phone back on campus. The cradle was pressed close to my ear and my voice was low, as the phone was situated in the middle of the hall where everyone could freely listen in.

I told the girl public phone calls weren't exactly private and asked if we could communicate via email instead. She said sure and asked if I had a pen ready.

"Wait, your middle name is *underscore*?" I asked her,

perplexed, as she gave me her e-digits. "That's a long email address," I commented further, looking at my notepad once I had it all down. She didn't email me back, but that didn't faze me, because soon after that phone conversation I fell hard for a fellow Oak Hill student, a girl on the basketball team a year younger than me. I could immediately tell that she was emotionally troubled which made me like her all the more, because I was troubled, too, subjected daily to a growing portfolio of obsessive-compulsive symptoms that I was too ignorant or scared to do anything about. Not that I had my finger on the subtleties of attraction at the time, as I was more concerned with her hair and her long legs and the sad way she floated around campus. She said she liked me back, and we went to prom together, and perhaps we crossed that imaginary line down the center of campus. I began to think about her all the time, quietly realizing that the anxious, superstitious nature of my mind stretched into girls too.

An entirely new love-related echelon of obsessive-compulsive symptoms took flight. She was a blanket, and I felt smothered by her and the symptoms I associated with her, whether or not she was around. The relationship, like so many of my relationships to come, was crippling to the point of debilitation, beyond any of the amorous extremes that are sometimes dramatically depicted in movies and books. My superstitions multiplied until pretty much every activity of my day was accompanied by a terrific panic as to whether or not the activity would boost or detract from the relationship. This was not teenage bliss. I lived with a constant cortisol drip, forever analyzing our every move and plotting the next one. I had no idea at the time that there was a term for this: ROCD, or Relationship

Obsessive-Compulsive Disorder.

At the end of the school year I was chosen to speak at graduation, but I didn't know myself well enough at eighteen to talk from the heart. I omitted reflective nuggets from my speech on our season (we finished No. 2 in the country) and avoided mention of the onerous trials of young love, infusing my talk instead with safe, myth-affirming clichés about the happy bright futures that awaited us all.

I was, however, aware that most students do not choose to uproot their hometown lives to attend a tiny boarding school in the middle of nowhere, and to this I said, "While we may not miss this place, we can be grateful for the ways that it took care of us while we were here." Indeed, while I didn't necessarily come out of my shell and fully flourish at Oak Hill, Coach Smith and his wife, Lisa, treated us like their own sons and gave us an unparalleled basketball experience. My teachers were attentive and engaged, and I did perhaps the most important thing I went there to do: ready myself for college.

By the end of my speech I was entirely comfortable at the podium, and I ad-libbed a lofty postscript, enjoying the sound of my voice booming out of the speakers on my flanks. When I finally finished, there was polite applause, and then a mass dispersal, and as I gathered my notes and dissolved into the crowd to find my family, I made the mistake of thinking it was the end of life's tough times.

Arriving at Davidson College in the fall of 2002, and despite my year at Oak Hill, I still had no idea how to define myself. This apparently wasn't anything abnormal, as *finding yourself* was a big theme at the freshmen-only, eve-of-first-day-of-classes assembly, where the college president allayed onsetting homesickness with a comedic welcome routine that was perhaps intended to remind us of our parents, and hence why we'd so long looked forward to college. It was the perfect time for self-discovery, he added when the jokes ran out, which was an inspiring proposition, but also confusing, as up until he mentioned it I hadn't realized I needed to be looked for. Oak Hill was the year I'd spent digging around under the existential couch cushions, the year I'd ripped myself away from family and hometown friends, the year I'd first learned how lonely the end of the bench can be, and the year my young heart was first flattened by the agitation called love. I wasn't so naive not to understand the president's implication, but, sitting with my hallmates in the audience, I nonetheless frowned and metaphorically thought, *but I'm right here*.

Part of finding yourself, I quickly learned, was sifting through the deluge of work that accompanies one's freshman year of college. Academia at Davidson proved to be a dense, unforgiving landscape, with esoteric vocabularies and persnickety class discussions, the points of which often seemed to have nothing to do with learning and more to do with disproving what other people thought they knew, in the most supercilious way possible. I was supposedly better prepared to contribute on the court — I was the crown of Davidson's freshman recruiting class, an Honorable Mention All-American who'd played alongside Carmelo at Oak Hill — but all the hype meant I had that much more to prove. It meant I'd meet that much more resistance from the incumbents whose spots in the lineup I was penciled in to take, upperclassmen who wasted no time pinballing me around the paint in preseason pick-up games.

Davidson is one of the premier liberal arts colleges in the world, a place where the term student-athlete is still fully applicable, but, as with any college, so much of a student-athlete's education has nothing to do with being a student or an athlete. I did not, at the time, have any idea how to politely tell my roommate to lock the door when he masturbated, or have any idea how to talk to girls who were mostly young women, or how to be 6'9" and sleep in a bed in a dorm designed in the 1950s. All around me, fellow freshmen were shedding their pre-collegiate skins and trying on new shades and colors, and I, too, experimented with new coats, trying in vain to find one that fit, trying to process all there was to learn. I learned the hard way that even if it tastes like tangy fruit juice, the burn as it trickles down your esophagus probably means you shouldn't drink it like you would a glass of Hawaiian Punch. I learned that intimacy isn't guaranteed when you get naked with someone and that closing one tired eye while you're studying doesn't mean extra lift for the other eye. "I" was apparently hidden somewhere in all this hubbub, but by the time I pulled on my No. 22 Davidson jersey in Duke's visiting locker room that November, I'd forgotten that I was supposed to be looking.

The Duke-Davidson game from November 2002 was good enough to open the 11 p.m. edition of ESPN's Sportscenter. We lost by double-digits, but had been within 6 with a minute to go, far closer than anyone expected going in. I scored 23 points and grabbed 6 boards against a top-five Duke team at Cameron Indoor Stadium on national television, easily one of my more personally distinguishable games ever. If I needed to find myself, there I was, on the screen and in the stat sheet, firmly enmeshed in the world of college basketball.

Returning to Davidson afterwards, I clicked open an inbox flooded with congratulatory emails. Returning to class the next Monday, girls seemed to recognize me, and some even smiled in my direction. Admirers jam-packed the dry-erase board on my dorm room door with messages, and even my roommate stopped masturbating long enough to wave with his free hand. Later that week Dick Vitale released a list of five promising freshmen for fans to keep an eye on, a list that included J.J. Redick, Sheldon Williams, Carmelo Anthony, Chris Bosh, and Ian Johnson. Four of those five players would go on to be lottery picks in the NBA.

In December that same year we played UNC-Charlotte, our crosstown rivals. The morning of the game the *Charlotte Observer* profiled me, and later that night I validated the attention with, among other highlights, a melted butter, so-good-it-looks-easy post move that made a statue of Charlotte's big-time center. In film session the next day, Coach McKillop wound and rewound the play, lauding it. Against Duke, I'd played freely and blankly, my mind so vacant that it didn't really feel like *me* playing. Watching Coach glorify me in film, I experienced the same sensation, feeling like I was watching someone else perform my moves. I stared at the screen, trying really hard to believe the good things Coach was saying. Coach wanted to praise me, but I didn't trust praise, and it was hard not to think that I was being set up, that my success to date was a conspiratorial hoax that everyone was in on but me, and that opposing teams had been deliberately playing beneath themselves to prop me up. Any moment, I knew, the gig would be up and everyone would have a good laugh at my expense.

Over Christmas break of that same year my team traveled to Tucson, Arizona for a holiday tournament, where we faced host Arizona in our opening match-up. Arizona, like Duke, was a top five team, but I still dropped 21 against a roster featuring future NBA stars Luke Walton and Channing Frye, who I repeatedly schooled on the low block.

Returning from Arizona, the coaching staff requested my presence at the gym. When I showed up, three assistants walked me into the empty arena, where we leaned against the scorer's table.

"Look up," they said. "See the jerseys?"

I looked up to the rafters, at the five numbers the school had retired to date, the oversized uniforms spaced evenly across a red beam. It wasn't a reverent gaze, as I knew nothing of their names or careers besides the blurbs they merited in our media guide.

"If you want it and work for it," the coaches said, "you'll see your name up there one day."

In 1946, the Basketball Association of America (BAA), the frontrunner to the NBA, was undergoing its own identity crisis. In late October, the New York Knicks were en route to Canada via train, where the following evening they were slated to play the Toronto Huskies in the league's first ever game. At Niagara Falls, a border agent, noticing the exceptional build of the men whose passports he was stamping, asked them, "What are you?"

"We're the New York Knicks," replied the Knicks' coach.

The border agent didn't know anything about the Knicks, or

even what sport they played, and proceeded to warn the players that nobody in Canada would care much either.

Professional basketball, post-WWII, was still trying to wriggle out of its chaotic dark ages, an era that had been defined largely by financial struggles, excessive roughness, and disputes about rules.

The man under whose tall torch pro basketball would finally find its footing was one George Mikan, a 6'10" bespectacled behemoth out of Depaul University. I grew up associating Mikan's name mostly with the Mikan drill (a repetitive right-to-left-to-right layup routine) and a few anachronistic black and white photos from the '50s that would occasionally get worked into modern media. It wasn't until I started writing this book that I began to understand the impact that he had on the NBA. (In 1949 the BAA would merge with the National Basketball League to form the National Basketball Association; the NBA folds the BAA's history into its own.)

Mikan was a talented big man when most big men to date had been stiffs. His proficiency with goaltending forced the league to legislate against it, and his dominance around the rim compelled the league to widen the lane. He was the game's first blanketing personality, the first "Mount Rushmorian" of a fledgling NBA that would flourish on individuality, as it still does today.

The college game has long thrived on individuality, as well, although it's often a coach's persona, not the player's, whose spotlight accrues the brightest glare. To many fans of my generation, a player's college career is merely a footnote in the broader discussion of that player's career in the NBA. Long-tenured campus coaches, however, provide continuity and emotional substance where eighteen year olds cannot. Bob Knight, Dean Smith, Mike Krzyzewski, Jim Boeheim, Adolph Rupp, Rick Pitino, Jim Calhoun, and John Wooden, to name but a few, are the most household of household names. For better or worse, it's their legacies that define the collegiate basketball landscape as much as, if not more so, any player's.

Sometime in February 2003, towards the end of my freshman season, I showed up at the gym on a day off and found my locker festooned with newspaper clippings. Highlighted in the articles were laudatory statements that various reporters and opposing coaches had made about me earlier in the year, and in the middle of the clippings was a handwritten note from Davidson's head coach and most towering personality, Bob McKillop. The note asked, "Where has this guy gone?"

It was a fair question. Our conference schedule, which began after the holidays, wasn't anywhere near as tough as our non-conference schedule. The crowds were smaller, and opposing rosters were no longer stacked with McDonald's All-Americans. If we played on television, it was a regional broadcast. Things should've been easier, but I still hadn't cracked the starting lineup, and, worse, I was no longer even such an immediate part of the rotation. Coach no longer exalted my post moves in film sessions; rather, he did quite the opposite, just as passionately, and with every tirade the idea that my jersey might one day hang in the rafters grew more remote. I had become a mess of contradiction, believing my hype at the same time I reacted against it, striving for superstardom while simultaneously wanting to hide. I still hadn't found myself, and felt more lost everyday, and it was impossible to think that someone with my troubled internal circuitry could be a superstar on a stage as big as college basketball. I'd come to think of myself as a fraud, which meant that my early-season success was fraudulent. How could I fully embrace a system that would let someone like *me* be successful?

Odd little compulsions had begun to unwittingly take over my life, with upgraded intensity. A few were familiar remnants from my youth — tapping my fingers in specific patterns, rigidly climbing stairs so that my right foot always reached the top step first — but these were harmless compared to a terrifying new wave of symptoms. I became violently obsessed, for instance, with the way I lined up my shoes at my dorm room door, sometimes getting out of bed in an insomniatic panic to adjust them in the middle of the night. Or there was the way I needed to look at a row of photographs in the arena's cafeteria a certain way, every time I saw them, my heart pounding with the fear that *not* looking at them the correct way would induce some horrific event. Then there was the way I tried to make sure I always stood at an appropriate angle to Coach when he was talking, usually to his right, as if that would determine what he might say. In order to keep this book to a reasonable word count, I'll stop listing the symptoms here, and you'll just have to believe me when I say the list of symptoms could fill a tomb.

To loop back around and answer Coach's question, where had that guy gone? The answer, I didn't want to admit, was nowhere, as he'd never truly been real. The narrative had flipped, but I no longer felt out of place, either. I no longer saw myself as a victim of identity theft, and I no longer felt like I'd been accidentally cast in the wrong movie.

Just a few years after inventing the game in 1891, James Naismith left Springfield for Colorado where he acquired a medical degree and officially added the title with which we so lovingly preface his name today. Then, in 1898, he became the first head coach at the University of Kansas (technically, Naismith was hired as a chapel director and a PE instructor), where he amassed a relatively dismal 55-60 record in eight seasons, the only coach in Kansas history to finish his career with a losing record. Among Naismith's lettermen during this tenure was one Forrest "Phog" Allen, an eager disciple of the game who tutored under Naismith's wing before busting out with his own agenda.

When we imagine basketball without coaches today, we think of pick-up, and apart from pick-up, there is no basketball without coaches. In the early 1900s, it was the other way around, and nobody is more responsible for the coming rise of the coach than Phog Allen. While Naismith saw basketball as a game in which the players, and only the players, should hold power — "you don't coach basketball; you just play it," he once said — Allen saw basketball as a game that should be coordinated from the sidelines. History doesn't portray Allen as an antagonist to Naismith, but in many ways Phog's foray into coaching was akin to outright defiance. Nonetheless, he is today universally crowned and celebrated as the "father of basketball coaching," his brushing aside of Naismith's founding philosophy notwithstanding.

Phog's coaching tactics were varied. Among many idiosyncrasies, he believed the warmth of one's feet was vital to good health, and would have his players sit with their toes to a fire for long stretches. In 1924 he published the prophetically titular *My Basket-ball Bible*, a 445-page compendium that covered coaching A to Z, 0 to 100, and all the sharps and flats in between, including sections about halftime entertainment, inspirational techniques, and even how to relieve hemorrhoids and jock itch (like Naismith, Phog had a medical degree). The book was a written declaration that basketball was evolving into something Naismith had never hoped nor expected it would become: a spectacle.

Before my first practice at Davidson, Coach McKillop, as he would go on to do every year, discussed with the team a paraphrased quote from Alexander Suvorov, the last generalissimo of the old Russian Empire: *difficult in training, easy in battle.* Coach McKillop was never a general and referred jock itch cases to the medical staff, but his coaching arsenal included something that neither Phog Allen nor Suvorov had access to, something both would have undoubtedly approved of: film.

Perhaps in no other profession besides porn or acting are one's performances so exquisitely scrutinized on tape as they are in sports. The Davidson film room in 2002 was a big windowless box, dug into the landscape like an underground bunker, with white-painted cinder block walls dotted with framed photos from championship seasons surrounding a diagram of a half-court sketched into the gray carpet. A big projector screen pulled down in front, and in a typical post-game session players filled the two rows of chairs closest to the screen while the assistant coaches hung out in the back and Coach McKillop assumed a clerical stance to the fore, remote in hand.

Coach McKillop was Coach with a capital C, respected in the community and on campus, around the conference, and across the country. While I was at Davidson, no professor, hallmate, friend, or teammate influenced my life like he did. No other voice was as authoritative or as loud, and that voice tended to operate on just two extremes. A box-out was "absolutely fantastic" or it was "simply atrocious"; an outlet pass was "outstanding" or it was "repugnant." There was little in between.

The lower the low points of my season dipped — a lackluster 10 points at Furman, a mere 6 at Georgia Southern, my scoring average struggling to stay in the double digits — the more I tended to hang out on a particular extreme of Coach's spectrum of analysis. Not knowing how to take or respond to his passionate brand of criticism, I forced myself not to react, and even when his delivery struck like a baseball bat to the temple, I never allowed him, or anyone else, to see the impact. I sat stone faced as he dissected our games, my stomach churning and armpits on fire, maintaining as perfectly passive an exterior as I could.

Coach McKillop's criticism of me was mostly in a basketball context, but, because basketball basically ruled my life then, and because what I thought of myself as a person depended on what I thought of myself as a player, and because what I thought of myself as a player depended on what Coach thought of me as a player, his assessments of me as a player became my overall assessments of myself as a whole person. If I just lost you with that sentence, consider that his station was the only one on the dial. The two hours a day I spent with him dictated my self-esteem across the other twenty-two.

Under the influence of both Coach McKillop and my festering obsessive-compulsive symptoms, my freshman year became, as it would throughout other parts of my career, a series of countdowns. I counted down the minutes to the end of practice, the days until the next day off, the hours to anything that wasn't happening *now*. But the harder I chased the future, the further away it got, and whenever anticipated moments actually arrived, I couldn't enjoy them because I was already counting down, much more dreadfully, to the start of the next practice, the next film session, or the next stretch of games.

Peace was impossible, but I did have a sustaining pastime. Every Thursday early afternoon, I'd pick up my *Sports Illustrated* from the post office in the Student Union. From there I would trek to the library and find a comfy chair behind the reference stacks, sink into the cushions, untie my shoelaces, and get lost, my contradictions calling a momentary truce while I dug into a new issue.

In March we were upset by VMI in the opening round of the Southern Conference Tournament. In the locker room after the game, several players wept openly, shedding tears I didn't understand. I watched the proceedings with detachment, returning the appropriate embrace when prompted, but otherwise just kind of sitting there trying to look and feel despondent because that's how I thought I should look and feel. But why? Sure, we had lost the game, and it *was* disappointing, but we'd just won our freedom too. No more practice. No more film. No more orange jumpsuit.

For a few shorts weeks anyway.

While back in Charlottesville for a quick break, I visited a bagel shop where my sister Hannah worked. She was behind the counter and I waved to her from my place in line. She waved back, but seemed intent on avoiding eye contact. When I tried to say hi, she mumbled an inaudible response and kept her head down. Confused, I collected my bagel and left.

At home, as if sensing my mood, my mom said, "You know, Ian, your sister is going through a tough time. Are *you* okay?"

I frowned as if she'd insulted me. "Am I okay?"

"It's okay if you're not okay."

"Mom, I'm fine. Relax."

"You sure?"

I might've rolled my eyes. "Yes, mom."

I wanted her to keep asking me if I was okay. If she had persisted, I would have eventually told her the truth.

My dorm room sophomore year was, amazingly, smaller than the one I'd lived in as a freshman, with cinder-block walls identical to those of the film room and furniture perhaps more suitable for the administration wing of a 1930s penitentiary. My desk chair could have been built by a Cub Scout, and my bed had a footboard that forced me to sleep curled up. Guys on my hall partied several nights a week, the thump of the bass nightly fluttering my eyelids like the water cup on the dashboard in *Jurassic Park* right before the T-Rex comes. The number I'd drawn in the dorm lottery the previous spring had been five from the bottom, which meant my room was literally one of the least desirable rooms on campus. The school was paying me $40k plus a year, and every material need was provided for, but in the context of affluent higher education it was hard not to feel sorry for myself.

The day I arrived back on campus, a few days before classes started, I trekked to the gym for a workout. Some minutes into my drills, Coach McKillop appeared at the lobby windows overlooking the near baseline where he watched for a minute before walking down to say hi. He asked how things were going, whether I had enjoyed my break, whether I was ready to build on my freshman year. We hadn't spoken since June, as I had chosen to spend the summer in Charlottesville and hadn't returned his calls. I told him it had been a productive few months, and to prove it I took my shirt off, unprompted, to show him all the weight and muscle I'd gained. Resuming my workout after he left, I suddenly felt dizzy and light-headed.

Later that week we gathered as a team in the weight room for a post-summer assessment session where I learned my bench press max had decreased by fifteen pounds since we'd last tested four months earlier. They kept having to take weight off the bar until I could get it up. Everyone else who wasn't injured had seen his max jump or at least stay the same. The coaches weren't thrilled with my numbers, as adding weight and muscle had been their primary summer goal for me, laid out in no uncertain terms the previous May.

But, no matter how sophomoric my shoulders, I still showed up at Davidson that August in incredible shape. My summer certainly hadn't been lazy. I'd put myself through grueling on-court workouts, complemented by sprints up vertiginous hills in the brutal Virginia heat. My summer, then, however industrious in certain areas, had been severely mismanaged elsewhere. I had no idea why.

My sophomore year unfolded the way my freshman year finished. From that very moment I ripped my shirt off for Coach McKillop, it was to his whims that my self esteem set sail everyday, and to his gales and breezes that that ship plotted its course. I was still struggling in the classroom and still getting banged up by the upperclassmen, although this time around I was less restrained in self-medication. Freshman year I'd mostly avoided alcohol. Sophomore year I learned how to take shots. Division I athletes apparently abuse alcohol more than any other campus demographic, a statistic I helped reinforce. I learned that if I drank enough, the obsessive-compulsive symptoms would often go away.

One afternoon, as I read alone in my dorm room, there came a knock at the door. It was a policeman, looking concerned.

"Just checking to see that you're okay?"

"Just fine, officer. Why do you ask?"

The night before, hanging out with people I didn't know very well, I'd gotten uproariously drunk with the sole intention of escaping my everyday mental state. Once I was good and wasted I ditched the group and wandered around alone, and sometime later the policeman had found me on the sidewalk, not far from a chunky puddle of my throw up, head between my knees, apparently unable to move. He'd led me back to my dorm and was there to make sure I was alright, but I could not recall him in the slightest. I thanked him for his concern, let him lecture me a bit on safe drinking habits, and sat down again with my book, staring blankly at the text, my heart undulating to an unsourceable tremor of disquiet.

I had teammates I liked and would grow to love, but I didn't know how to show myself to any of them. Perhaps due to the lingering effects of getting bullied as a kid, I was afraid to engage them in a sincere conversation. Instead, I acted cocky and goofy and non-threatening, knowing that people feel better about themselves when other people play the fool.

My second college summer, the one before my junior year, was more productive than the first. I stayed on campus and, making up for lost time, spent long hours in the weight room and ballooned my daily caloric intake. Every night before bed I wolfed down two thick peanut butter sandwiches. A side dish for dinner was often a box of mac and cheese.

By the end of the summer I'd put on almost forty pounds — thirteen a month if you're keeping score — and this time around in pre-season assessment I showed off massive gains. This included my body fat, which jumped to nearly fifteen percent, up from six percent the previous spring. My body had transformed, but I'd overshot my goals and ended up overweight.

As my junior year began, I still hadn't worked through, or even acknowledged, my growing portfolio of obsessive-compulsive symptoms. That fall, as we did every pre-season, we played pick-up three or four times a week. The games were heated, as pick-up games with young men usually are. We called our own fouls, which allowed for all kinds of macho posturing when a dispute arose. One particular game was tied 6-6, playing to 7, when the ball was knocked out of bounds. I had been the last to touch it but I pretended I hadn't, which set off an impassioned feud for possession, with lots of ball-slamming and dramatic shows of incredulity and dialogue heavy with variations of "you're full of shit." My team eventually won the ball, and the next time down on offense I hit the game-winner.

In the locker room afterwards, as we peeled off our wet socks and turned up Biggie and taped ice bags to our knees, I started to feel guilty. I'd lied. It should've been their ball. By the time we were all sitting down to flank steaks and steak fries in the cafeteria, the guilt had ratcheted up to a point where it was impossible for me to think of anything else. It felt like a thousand angry hornets were protesting in my synapses, the buzz crescendoing like Hans Zimmer's sustained siren in *The Dark Knight*. I'd planned to hit up the library and do a little work after dinner, but instead I retreated to my room, where I forced myself to lay down and not move, so fearful that I'd jump out the window or slam my temple against the corner of the desk. Feeling guilty about a small lie is normal, but entertaining suicidal thoughts about a small lie is something else.

During one practice at the dawn of our conference season, we were on the court running drills following a lengthy, energy-sapping film session. The big guys were doing high post drills, and as I waited in line at the elbow, Coach McKillop strode up and told me, very matter-of-factly, to start thinking of a list of five schools that I'd be willing to transfer to. His intention was debatable — maybe he was just trying to motivate me — but my reaction was not. Tears assumed battle stations in my eyes and my throat tightened, an emotional release ready for deployment, and it took a herculean effort to keep it all from spilling forth. I ignored him and tried to get on with the drill, but Coach followed me around, telling me he'd be more than happy to make calls to other coaches on my behalf. *You're not welcome here anymore*, is the message I got. It was as close as I would ever come to breaking, but still I did not crack. I considered my unbreakable facade some sort of accomplishment but, if I never cracked, nothing could change.

The Battle of Bunker Hill, one of the earliest conflicts of the Revolutionary War, was fought in June of 1775 near Charlestown, just outside Boston, Massachusetts. Leading the rebel forces that summer day was Colonel William Prescott, who, with his men short on ammunition, is historically noted for having given the famous command not to fire until his soldiers could see the whites of the enemy eyes. Like many American students who strive for good grades in history class, I proudly digested this information upon its receipt and for years kept it safe on the mantle of my inner patriotism. It was not without a strange wave of dissonance that I later learned that not only did the American rebels lose the Battle of Bunker Hill, but that the battle wasn't actually fought on Bunker Hill, and nobody knows for sure if it was actually Prescott who gave the order not to fire until one could make eye contact with the enemy.

Among the men who indisputably did battle with Prescott at Bunker Hill in 1775 was a man named Barzillai Lew. Some thirty miles from Bunker Hill, in Lowell, Massachusetts, and 127 years later in 1904, Barzillai's eighteen-year old great-great-great grandson, Bucky Lew, sat on the bench and watched his teammates on the Pawtucketville Athletic Club basketball team play a squad from Marlborough in the young New England Basketball League, one of several professional fledgling leagues sweeping across the Northeastern landscape at the time.

Bucky wasn't expected to get in the game, as he was there more to fill out the roster and collect five dollars for doing so. But one of Bucky's teammates got hurt, which left his team playing four on five, and so into the game Bucky went. Bucky, like his great grandfather Barzillai, was African-American, which made Bucky the first black man to integrate a professional basketball league in the United States. The story of Bucky Lew — and that of the New York Renaissance and the Harlem Globetrotters and many other African-American pioneers — is told in most of the basketball history books that I read in researching this one. Some authors, I found, tend to present stories like Lew's, and that of basketball's eventual full-scale integration in the 1940s, as more of a celebratory event, a triumph of the American system. They point out how multiple black players participated in white leagues in 1942-43, a five full years before Jackie Robinson broke baseball's color line, and they also point to the relative lack of drama surrounding Earl Lloyd's debut with the Washington Capitals, the first time a black player took the floor in the NBA, on Halloween night in 1950. Conversely, other basketball histories present the story of integration as more of a triumph against a vast, deeply ingrained system of American oppression. They freely dive into the rampant abuse and bias faced by the black players of the game's early eras, even as those players were making history.

My own story, the one I'm telling here in this book, has its own trove of divided historians. All are rooted inside my own head, and each is intent on telling my story a certain way. One part of me, for instance, wants to paint my career in the most flattering light possible, while another part of me knows that being vulnerable and open about my struggles is the only way to truly relate to readers. It's gotten loud between my ears, but I consider having conflicting historians in the room an accomplishment unto itself, as most of the time, for most of my life, the only narrative I would entertain, at any juncture, was *I'm perfectly fine*, and at no point in my career was the impulse to stoke that narrative higher than at the end of my junior year at Davidson, when I most needed to accept the opposite.

A couple weeks after our season ended with a loss to Maryland in the NIT, during a time away from basketball when I was supposedly "free," I sat next to a teammate in a computer lab watching a video called *Non-Olympians*. There was a woman tripping over her javelin mid-stride, a not-so-coordinated pole-vaulter, and a hurdler tumbling over the blocks. I was amused and my teammate was laughing, yet I was also looking at him and thinking, *Man, he doesn't see,* and from there my thoughts spiraled into someplace dark. *He doesn't see, nobody has ever seen, I have to do something about this.* My struggles on the court and my omnipresent obsessive-compulsive symptoms were beyond overwhelming, a condition amplified by my inability to tell anyone, anyone at all, including myself, that I wasn't okay.

I grabbed my backpack and left the computer lab. It was early evening and the air was warm, the kind of sun-kissed warmth that feels like a Coca-Cola commercial. I walked slowly towards my car, keys rotating on my finger, thinking how wonderful it was to feel warm like that. I was aware that something was going to happen, something that could make everything go away forever, and a few minutes later I had an explicit plan. It was a plan I'd apparently been ruminating on for some time, as the details already seemed to be in place. My plan was this: I would drive to the Home Depot and buy a couple of cement blocks and some rope. If the Home Depot didn't sell cement blocks, I'd grab a few dumbbells from the weight room. Then I'd drive to nearby Lake Norman, walk out on the dock, tie one end of the rope to the blocks and the other to my ankles, and jump in.

I was excited yet calm at the thought of death, feeling like I was about to go on a long vacation. I was more than desperate enough to execute my plan, but a dissenting member of my internal Congress was ringing alarms and screaming for me to hang on. Acquiescing to the minority whip, I decided to give myself a chance. I would make one phone call, and if I got through to someone, I'd consider aborting my termination. But to give myself a chance, I needed to do something I'd never done before: reach out. I cycled through the contact list in my phone and settled on one of our assistant coaches, Matt Matheny. "I need to come over," I said when he answered.

Before I could talk myself out of it, I drove to Matt's house in a nearby neighborhood where he plopped me down in an easy chair and set a glass of water at my side. I was sobbing before I could give him any explanation for my visit, sobs so intense they sapped me of breath and left me gasping, which was probably all the explanation he needed. When I finally settled down I found I had nothing to say. I didn't know what was wrong, only that something was.

"I'm fucked up," was all that I could get out.

Matt suggested I talk with my parents. I told him I would, then thanked him and drove back to my apartment on campus. My roommate, Clu, was watching television.

"What's up, man?" he asked when I walked in.

"Chillin', man," I replied.

My night with Matt had been cathartic, almost euphoric, but the endorphins were temporary. Less than a week later I was up late on the eve of my twenty-first birthday, a birthday that supposedly marked my coming of age, sitting shirtless at the small desk in my small room, pocket knife in hand. The blade was drawn and held to the crevice between my ribs, the desperation to end my life so great that the thought of driving all the way to the Home Depot seemed too much to bear. I hadn't called my parents, like I'd promised, nor had I over the previous days taken any other steps to mitigate my desire to self-cancel. When the urgency overwhelmed me again, worse than at the computer lab, I simply went into my room, closed the door, and grabbed the most readily available option. This time I wasn't calm and excited; I was insane. I had no idea what was happening, no idea how to make sense of my brain, which had become a cauldron of boiling thoughts, a million pistons in a thousand cars accelerating at the sight of a frantic green flag, always ready to run an endless race on a darkened decrepit track.

The knife was old and the blade beginning to rust. Failing to break the skin, I tried again, this time looking up towards the ceiling. I tried next with two hands, my face clenched with effort, sweat cracking my forehead, but couldn't induce a thrust. It didn't occur to me to slit my wrists, but even if it had, I probably wouldn't have done it. My emotional eruption with Matt had broken some important seal, taking with it the resolve I'd felt after leaving the computer lab. I didn't, therefore, feel compelled to consider any sort of suicide note, but if I'd written one, it might have gone like this:

Dear Confusing World,

I'm so stopped up with repressed emotion and so exhausted with faking my confidence that I'm willing to do pretty much anything to make it all go away, including stabbing myself with a pocket knife. You see, pretty much every male role model in my life, from my dad to my coaches, has either directly or indirectly told me that emotional expression is for girls, and girls only. I'm supposed to be passionate, sure, but not a pussy. This has made my life hard, because there's a lot I really need to get out, or even just tell someone about, but it seems like the only way I can tell anyone that I'm not okay is in a letter that nobody will read until I'm gone. I wish the world wasn't this way, but it is, and so I must take leave of it. Goodbye.

Thankfully, I never needed to write such a letter, and instead of stabbing myself I sheathed the knife and collapsed on my bed, where I instantaneously drifted into death's closest approximation.

In the late seventies, Dave Cowens, a star center for the Boston Celtics who would be inducted into the Hall of Fame in 1991, abruptly paused his NBA career and started driving a cab, an occupational pivot that has become NBA lore. Ex-coach and current television analyst Jeff Van Gundy, during a live broadcast in 2009, commented "Cowens was always my favorite player. Do you think any of these players today would stop playing basketball and go drive a cab for a living?"

It's a fascinating anecdote to contemplate — one of the league's best players for one of the league's most storied teams taking a break from the game to ferry tourists to Fenway Park — except it's not really true. Cowens did drive a cab in the 70s, except just for one night — you could apparently do this back then — and only as a unique way to show a visiting buddy around the city.

But another Dave Cowens comeback story, a real one, goes like this: In 1975-76, Cowens' averaged 19 points and 16 rebounds in helping lead Boston to the NBA title. As the 76-77 season began, however, Cowens' wasn't sure if he wanted to play anymore, for reasons that had nothing to do with driving a taxi. In a 2010 interview with *The Huffington Post*, Cowens said, "I just got burned out on basketball. I didn't care to compete anymore. I wasn't the most talented guy around, so I had to give it that big effort just to play against an average guy."

Cowens asked for and received permission from Boston GM Red Auerbach to take a break from the game. He spent time at his family farm in Kentucky, selling Christmas trees, but a few months later he returned to the court, resuming a career that would ultimately land him on the NBA's 50 All-Time Greatest Players List, coming back not from injury or a scoreboard deficit, but from a retreat of the mind and will. If I wanted to keep living following my junior year, I would have to do much of the same.

If you have the credits, Davidson seniors can take one less class during their final spring semester. I didn't have the credits, nor did I want a full course load come spring, so the summer before my senior year I emailed a psychology professor and seemingly at random proposed a topic for a summer course: mental illness in athletes.

The professor and I met once a week in his office and spent much of our time together discussing the research, but by the end of the hour the professor's pen was always down. He'd have me put my notes away, and he'd diagonally find a way to ask how I related to the material.

"Um, it reads like a diary," I didn't say but could have. I saw so much of myself in the anonymous case studies I read about — self-sabotage, suffocating superstitions, total assimilation of sport and self — although I couldn't have told you that at the time. I was fascinated by the subject but I didn't think it was personal. I considered the class an academic foray along one of sports' outer lanes, conducted the way a pastry chef might play around with a wok in his free time.

In retrospect I realize, of course, that my summer class was therapy, that the professor, a practicing psychiatrist, was doing me a favor, forcing me to personalize my research and therefore confront, however indirectly, the dysphoric depths of my situation. This was Davidson being Davidson, providing a confused but willing student with the resources to educate himself in the most important of ways. I'd watched other students design their own courses, even their own majors, and been both envious and scared of their self-initiative. I'd now found the courage to do something similar myself, and I was finally beginning to understand what the school president had meant in his welcome speech three years before.

It worked. Within six weeks or so, I suddenly had a brief but relatively accurate academic narrative of a good chunk of my life. More importantly, I had someone safe with whom to talk, and that summer, my last as a collegiate athlete, was finally as productive as I needed it to be. My weight stabilized at 225 pounds, a healthy playing weight I'd keep for the remainder of my career. My roommate Clu and I moved into a spacious (by college standards) apartment near the admissions building, and for the first time in college I wasn't sleeping on a single bed in a noisy concrete-walled dorm room. I had real privacy, and, perhaps most crucially, I lived off-campus; I could leave Davidson grounds every single day. How important this was to my mental health is hard to quantify, and how important my mental health was to the success of my senior season is almost impossible to underestimate.

In August of that same summer my team flew to Europe for a two-week exhibition tour. On the last night of our stay, in Treviso, near Venice, Italy, stumbling back to the hotel hours past curfew, I held my teammates up near a pedestrian bridge arching over an ancient canal. The streetlights made slightly nauseating cones of yellow on the cobblestones, the walls of the adjacent buildings condensing our world to the circumference of our revelry. I motioned for us to huddle up, draped my arms around the guys to my left and right, and felt a pair of arms lay across my own shoulders.

"Guys," I said, slurring a little, "this is the time of our fucking lives."

The response was riotous. We had just spent two weeks trying to get accustomed to European referees, learning how to pour wine and posing shirtless in the Alps. In the morning we would fly back to Davidson. Life was good.

"No, for real man," I continued, hushing everyone again. "This whole year is going to be the fucking *time of our lives.*"

The moment was the coronation of my transformative summer. I don't know if I was happy, but I wasn't suicidal anymore, either, and that certainly counts for something. I could a see a future with me in it, and if I wasn't ready for happiness I could settle for being optimistic.

I averaged 16 points and 6 rebounds my senior year, easily my best season at Davidson. I was no longer so dissonant with my dissonance and my contradictions were no longer so contradictory. Building on my summer course, I started speaking up in class, and I no longer found the academic landscape so unforgiving. I still hated film and Coach still made dents in me, but I no longer relied on him so heavily to establish a sense of self. I joined a couple clubs and made friends with non-teammates, and Clu and I smoked the field on our way to winning a months-long, campus-wide beer pong tournament, all of it proving, in the end, the prescience of my presumption in Treviso.

We played the Citadel in the opening round of the year-end conference tournament. Despite trailing by 17 late in the first half, we clawed our way back and won, advancing to the semifinals. Watching film afterwards back in the hotel, Coach paused the tape in the midst of our rally. We'd just scored a huge bucket, plus the foul.

"Now watch Ian here," he said, starting the tape again, and we watched as I threw my arm forward following the made shot. Not quite a fist pump, but at the very least its cousin.

"That's a lot of emotion from you, Ian," Coach said, looking at me as if demanding an explanation. For some length of time Coach rewound and replayed my quasi-celebration, just like he'd done with my early highlights as a freshman. That faux fist pump was a lot of emotion from me indeed, maybe the most emotion I'd ever displayed in a Davidson uniform. In fact, it might've represented *all* the emotion I'd *ever* displayed in a Davidson uniform, in nearly four

60

seasons.

We beat Elon in the semis and crushed Chattanooga in the final, securing the Southern Conference championship and clicking our ticket to the NCAA tournament.

A few days before tournament play started, I ventured into the Student Union to check my mail, included in which was *Sports Illustrated's* annual NCAA tournament preview issue. Back then one player from each participating team made the cover, and that evening when I took my copy to the library I settled into a chair between the reference stacks and stared down at my own tiny portrait, just beneath the double-L in Illustrated, my face grimacing as I snatched a rebound, my left nipple half-visible.

We were slated to play 2nd-seed Ohio State, in Dayton, Ohio, on CBS, in the 12:00pm game on that first Friday of the tournament. We bullied our way to a 29-25 halftime lead, but OSU came back and scratched out a 81-73 victory. I scored 26 points and grabbed 10 rebounds, the 26 a career high at the time, and despite the loss I was named Chevrolet Player of the Game. I cried as I walked off the court, a rush of emotion I was still too self-unaware to understand.

A month later, on a Sunday morning in May, I walked across the stage at the Davidson's Belk Arena, shook the school president's hand and accepted a diploma. The president smiled and said congratulations, but didn't follow up on the speech he'd given us four years earlier.

The summer after graduation, after I'd signed with Mike and begun to turn my attention to Europe, I sat with a few ex-teammates and incoming recruits in a Davidson apartment and watched the American men's soccer team compete in the World Cup. One of our recruits was a skinny kid from Charlotte, North Carolina named Stephen Curry. When a couple of upperclassmen arrived to the apartment late, Curry moved from the couch and sat on the floor to make room. He didn't say much throughout the game, and when he did say something he spoke so softly I couldn't understand him.

That night we all played pick-up, and there was one sequence where Steph drove from the top of key to the high post, where I switched onto him. He pivoted and made contact, stopping my momentum, then pivoted back the way he came and drained a 15-foot jumper. I remember being quietly surprised, almost stunned, at both the IQ and execution of a such a move

I wasn't the only one who was seeing things in him. Before his freshman season the following August, Coach McKillop met with several of our boosters and informed them that our program was about to change. When I heard about this meeting, I couldn't help but take it personally.

Chapter 3 — Indoctrination Part Three

In Spain in late November 2006, four months after I told Jesus at the team dinner that I loved everything about Gijon, I found myself at another restaurant by the water, this time alone. It wasn't a team dinner and there was no raucous sidra-pouring, no vodka shots or troupe of wives and girlfriends.

We had a game the night before and lost pathetically, Diego flailing on the sideline like a deranged conductor directing a symphony of dogs. I'd started the game, played about four minutes, then was pulled and sat the rest of it on the bench where I forced myself to cheer half-heartedly. But, because I wasn't playing, I was secretly hoping we would lose. By this point, I was a mere wisp of the athlete I'd been at Davidson the year before, the guy who'd thrived on national television, the guy who regularly dropped 20 points against ranked opponents and in tournament play. My summer course with the psychology professor had done me wonders, but it was just a scratch in the armor of my pathology. In Gijon, as I sat down at the restaurant by myself, by now very accustomed to eating alone, I'd retreated into the awful but familiar dark places of my mind.

After our loss Diego had reluctantly given us a day off, which I spent wandering around down by the Bay of Biscay, meandering up and down the shoreline before venturing up some nearby hills. A cold, salty spray carbonated my face as I squatted and gazed out over the water. The bay was expansive and dropped mystically off the horizon, and in another circumstance such a sight would have invoked within me feelings of infinity and awe, but in my current situation I was feeling more like the water itself, gray, bleak, and troubled. When I became hungry, I found a little Italian restaurant down a cobblestone alley with red-and-white checkered tablecloths covering a cramped but cozy arrangement of rickety wooden tables. I ordered fish and a pitcher of sangria. A newspaper floated amongst the tables, which I grabbed and aligned next to my bottle of mineral water.

My pitcher of sangria arrived, dark purple and thick with citrus slices. The waiter, a portly man with an I-really-have-better-things-to-do-now-than-serve-you demeanor, poured me a glass. I took a sip and tried to relax, but I'd been having trouble relaxing, hence the sangria.

There was a lot I wanted the alcohol to help me forget. Preseason was an absurdly trying seven weeks of monotonous two-a-days. For comparison, NBA training camps are a little more than a few weeks, and the NCAA allows three or four, maximum. If I had to list the ten worst weeks of my life, all seven preseason weeks in Gijon would probably make it.

The other American on our team, Jason, arrived five or so weeks into preseason, having been allowed to stay in the States longer than me because his wife had recently given birth to a baby boy. Jason stayed one night in that dank, dark, abandoned apartment, the one I'd stayed in upon my arrival, before demanding to be moved.

"How in the world did you spend a month in that place?" he asked me, bewildered, during our first conversation.

"Yeah, it wasn't that great," I said, which was the closest I could come to admitting how awful it really was.

But I had been moved, eventually, to a nicer apartment across town, much closer to the arena. Unfortunately my obsessive-compulsive symptoms packed up and moved too, and made themselves at home in my new digs.

My performances on the court, excluding the occasional day when I somehow turned it on, had steadily deteriorated over those first seven weeks. I wasn't awful (yet) but I was definitely not living up to the high standards set for American imports.

I scored just 5 points in our first game. We lost. I didn't even start. Diego laid into the team in the locker room afterwards, thrashing around like one of those inflatable creatures you see outside department stores, juking and bobbing in the wind. We had little cohesion and morale sucked, and even though we practiced together every day, nobody knew who anybody else was, at least not enough to build any sort of requisite trust or cooperative framework. That first team dinner was the only one we ever had. By November we'd sunk to the bottom of the league, low enough to arouse fears of relegation.

For a while my performances hovered on the low cusp of acceptable, and there were perhaps flashes of the player they were paying me to be. But overall I was an enigma, clearly capable, but somehow incapable of letting it all out. Simple things, like layups, began to require excessive concentration and effort. I started forgetting plays, and no matter how hard I tried, I couldn't relearn them.

During one game, while the other team was shooting free throws, I suddenly became scared that I wouldn't remember the ensuing play, even before I knew what that play was. I beckoned to our point guard and frantically implored him to tell me what play we were going to run so I could rehearse, but he just frowned and made a palms-down motion, as if to say *chill*.

As he dribbled the ball up the court I ran beside him, yelling "Que? Que?" As he crossed half court he called out a set, a play we'd run hundreds of times in practice, but one that I couldn't recall no matter how viciously I racked my brain. Panicking, I ran to the high post and looked around, hoping someone would settle for a quick shot. Some seconds later Diego was yelling at me from the sidelines, and I spun this way and that, like a drunk stumbling around a crowded bar, unsure of where to go or what to do. At the next dead ball, Diego subbed me out staring at me confusedly as I made my way to the bench. I looked at him with wide eyes and shrugging eyebrows, as if to say *I have no idea, either*.

I wasn't drunk that game, but alone at that little restaurant by the water, I was on my way. I finished my glass of sangria and poured another. A few minutes later the waiter set my fish down with a clatter, and I spent several minutes scraping the white, flakey flesh off the bones. Finally satisfied, I slid my plate onto the newspaper, which I'd opened to the sports section, where the lead article was from our game the previous night.

An object seen with the naked eye looks vastly different than when seen through a microscope or a telescope. A collection of dots is just a collection of dots, but zoom out a little and those dots become the pixels that form a line of text, until you zoom out even more and can no longer even see the newspaper. From a sentimental perspective,

Ernest Hemingway's time in Spain in the mid-1930s was legendary, filled with the kind of adventure and love that impressionable young men like myself often idolize. I read *The Sun Also Rises* when I was living in Spain, and, like so many before me, after completing it I grew worried that my life would never be as romantic and carefree as Hemingway's was depicted in the book. After *The Sun Also Rises* I read *For Whom the Bell Tolls*, and the tears that slid down my cheeks when I completed the book were the first time a piece of art ever made me cry. But was I crying in sympathy with Robert Jordan, the book's main character, or because the writing had exposed some sad void in my own life, particularly in comparison to Hemingway's? Hemingway is rightly revered for forever changing the way we write, but zoom out a little and see that with different magnifications Hemingway's time in Spain wasn't quite as pleasantly symphonic as his legend would have us believe. Various accounts of his time with the rebellious Republican forces paint Hemingway as "a joke," a foreign intellectual intent on seeing the political circumstances only as he wanted to see them, and Hemingway met and carried on an affair in Madrid with his future wife, Martha Gellhorn, while married to his second wife, Pauline Pfeiffer, who he met and whom he had an affair with while married to his first wife, Hadley Richardson, back in Paris in the 1920s. He was either a passionate lover, a hunter of wild game, a man who loved to play hard, or he was a misogynistic homophobe and alcoholic serial adulterer who murdered animals for fun.

"Are you actually reading that?" asked Claire, a character in Pulitzer Prize-winning author Jeffrey Eugenides' 2011 masterpiece *The Marriage Plot*, when she saw the book's protagonist, Mitchell, reading and admiring *A Moveable*

67

Feast. "Hemingway?" she said, dubiously.

Hemingway had the luxury of letting his work speak for itself, but since my performances on the court in Gijon weren't particularly voluminous (discounting my chaotic internal monologue) or impactful (10 points was my season high), Gijon's journalists were compelled to take up the task for me. The article I read in the restaurant began like this:

"Basketball is a game dictated by fairness and rules. No matter the disparity in talent, it is only fair that both teams should begin each game with an equal number of players on the court. Yet somehow Gijon miscounted and a number of minutes passed before Diego realized his error. Correcting, he pulled Ian Johnson from the lineup and substituted in another, at which point the game began in earnest, played as it should be, five on five."

I read this opening paragraph, absently, a number of times, unsure how to process. It was undoubtedly disconcerting to read about myself in such terms, but it was also puzzling, full of a peculiar dissonance. Here was Gijon's most popular newspaper devoting hundreds of words to my denigration. Whoever wrote the article would have thought about me for much of its construction. Somebody's job had been, for a night at least, to come up with ways to relay in writing my ineptitude. It was oddly flattering.

Engrossed by the article, I hadn't touched my fish. Then, having read the article, I assumed the waiter had read it too, and I assumed he recognized me as its principal subject. Assuming this, I could no longer eat my meal in peace so I wolfed it down and paid the bill, making sure to cover any inconveniences I might have created with my presence by leaving a big tip.

The call came a week later, in early December. It was Mike.

"They're going to make a change," were his words, coldly transcontinental from New York. "You're out, Ian."

I was being cut.

Mike gave me the details of my dismissal, including the pecuniary terms. In addition to all the money I'd made so far, the team would give me two additional months of salary *not* to play for them anymore. This seemed excessive, as I wouldn't have minded being cut for free.

"Stay in Europe as long as you can," Mike said. "It's easier to get you another job if you're already over there."

Hanging up the phone I felt lighter, almost giddy, like I had to hold on to something to keep from skittering around like a June bug.

Someone from the team called a few minutes later and asked if I would meet with the media.

"Right now?"

"Si."

Drenched in a mysterious, almost euphoric brand of melancholy, I drove to the arena and spoke for thirty minutes with a couple of radio stations and a few newspaper guys, all in fluent Spanish, my grasp of the language suddenly pristine. I told them I had no idea why I hadn't adjusted the way everyone had hoped, that I was just as mystified as everyone else as to my poor play, that Gijon was a great city and that Gijon Baloncesto was a great organization, that everything had been great, great, great.

From the arena I was off to the airport to pick up my mom and older sister, Hannah, who happened to have landed in Gijon that very night, in town to see me hoop it up.

It took me awhile to get it all out.

"I've got some good news and some bad news," is what I finally said, accelerating on the expressway, the twinkling lights of Gijon growing larger through the windshield. My mother looked over, folding her hands on her lap, her way of containing worry. "What's up?"

"Well, the good news is I'll get to do a lot of sightseeing with you guys." I paused here, moving my jaw back and forth, unsure of what to say next. "And you can still go to the game if you want. I just won't be playing."

Before leaving Gijon to tour Spain with my mom and Hannah, I stopped by the arena to grab my gear. I ran into Diego outside his office. He was glowing, not trying to hide the ways my departure had energized him. The team had just signed another American and a rush of optimism was in the air. I knew he blamed me for the team's downslide, first privately and then publicly, in a series of passive-then-not-so-passive-aggressive quotes that I couldn't help searching for everyday in the newspapers.

Hannah arrived in Spain with news of her own: she was sober. A few months before, she'd entered a thirty-day outpatient program but had sabotaged herself on the last day. A week or so later, she tried again and this time made

70

it through. In Spain she'd been sober two months, and nightly took Disulfiram, a chemical that was perilous when mixed with alcohol. She was raw and exhausted the whole trip, but driving through Bilbao, Oviedo, and Santander with her, I was, in a way, hanging out with my sister for the first time since I was eleven.

A few weeks later, I was in Virginia at my parent's house waiting for a call from Mike. In between workouts I attended Alcoholics Anonymous meetings with Hannah. Most of the people who shared spoke about their lives with a brutal and unfiltered honesty. They admitted their weaknesses, which somehow made them stronger. They talked about surrendering to their personal versions of a higher power, which somehow made them more powerful. I understood for the first time that Hannah was an alcoholic and an addict, and that there was an entire wealth of vocabulary to describe her condition. She and the others knew exactly who they were — "I'm an alcoholic" — and I envied them for it. When the meetings ended, my obsessive-compulsive symptoms often took a break.

Mike called the day after Christmas and told me a team in the Czech Republic wanted to give me a shot. He pushed for me to take the deal. It was less money in a lesser league, but it was that or nothing.

After hanging up the phone, I went upstairs to my bedroom and pulled out my map. I crouched down on my knees and unrolled it across the bed, finding Europe and then the Czech Republic. I set my finger down and stared, less idealistically, more suspiciously, at the places I'd go.

Chapter 4 — Addiction Part One

I was slouched at the kitchen table, absently scanning the box scores of the holiday tournaments I used to play in, when the phone's ring pierced the mid-morning calm in my parents' home in Virginia.

My mother, busy with yuletide cookie cutters at the counter, wiped her hands on a nearby dishtowel and answered. Fingers over the speaker, a curious frown on her forehead, she looked at me and said "For you. Some guy named Dalek calling from the Czech Republic."

I pushed myself back from the table and held out my hand, the moisture already accumulating on my outstretched palm.

"This is Ian."

It was late December 2006, a few days after Christmas, and I'd been back from Spain for almost a week, making the rounds with family and friends, trying to explain why I was unexpectedly home and being vague about when I would go back overseas.

Dalek introduced himself as the general manager for a team in Liberec, a city one hundred kilometers north of Prague, whose basketball team, the Condors (Kondori), at the time of the phone call, were in 9th place in the Czech Narodni Basketbalova Liga. They were looking to sign an American big man for the second half of the season and he was calling to feel me out.

"So what happened in Gijon?" Dalek asked me.

"I'm not sure," I said, which was the truth. "Things just didn't work out."

"Are you in shape?"

"I think so."

"Good."

The phone rang again later that afternoon, this time it was Mike calling from New York.

"Liberec wants you," he said, but a skeptical Dalek was insisting on a two-week tryout period before they'd sign me for the rest of the season; if the team didn't like me they had fourteen days to give me the axe.

Scanning the thick bilingual contract that Mike faxed me later that evening, I couldn't pick out more than a few words on the diacritic-heavy Czech side — Ceska Republika, auto, and dolar. Even with the English translation it sort of felt like I was blindly initialing a protracted "I've read and agree to all terms and conditions" box, signing away the next months of my life to strangers in a strange land, which, in a way, I was.

Before I left again for Europe, and just like I'd done with Spain, I unrolled my big laminated world map across my bed. I located the Czech Republic, eyeballing the yolk-yellow smudge in low center Europe as if the map might have something to say. But after Spain I knew better than to stare too long, so I made the map a scroll again and shoved it back into my closet.

On December 30th, 2006, I crossed the Atlantic en route

to Vienna, Austria. Settling into my seat, I thought of the flight attendant from my maiden trip to Spain. Illogically, I peeked around the cabin, just in case she was on board, although I couldn't even remember what she looked like.

From Vienna I puddle-jumped to Prague, where Dalek picked me up at the airport (on time!). He had one of those motel-issued baggage trolleys onto which I dropped my single suitcase, which wasn't, quite noticeably, all that full, the front flap sinking into itself like a hollow cheek. If not for my basketball shoes, I probably could've gotten by with a couple of carry-ons.

"Is that all you got?" Dalek asked.

I glanced down at my suitcase, trying to understand what he meant.

We loaded ourselves into Dalek's car and worked our way out into the flow of Skodas and Alfa Romeos, my adventure in the Czech Republic officially underway. Dalek was somehow just like I'd pictured: slightly suspicious looking, robotic, and serious. As we zoomed up an overpass on the E-65, Prague proper unfolded out the window to my left. Dalek wasn't from Prague, but, like every other Czech citizen I met, he had both connections to and opinions about the historic city. He explained the duality of the Czech Republic: there was Prague, and then there was Everywhere Else. Citizens from Everywhere Else weren't particularly fond of Prague, maybe because, according to Dalek, the people of Prague didn't particularly care for the citizens of Everywhere Else. But Prague was, and is, the point guard of the Czech Republic, dictating the cultural and economic offense for the rest of the country. I decided I liked Prague.

We stopped for lunch at an IKEA cafeteria in some grey suburb just off the highway. While we ate, I further studied Dalek. His sternness, particularly the semi-slitted eyes and perpetual mini-flare of the nostrils, made him look like he was always on the verge of a sneeze, like some over-caffeinated Scrooge at middle age. I decided I wasn't sure what to make of Dalek.

Three-quarters of a millennia old, Liberec was once the "Manchester of Bohemia," home to a thriving textile industry. It is, like a lot of European cities, better known for its history than its current iteration, a description that, after Gijon, neatly summed up my basketball career.

Dalek dropped me at a hotel near the sports arena, where I'd stay until my tryout ended. "Rest up," he said, and told me to be at the practice facility the following morning at nine. He handed me some Czech bills and wished me a happy new year.

Later that afternoon, as a descending black chased the last scars of pinkish-yellow from the cold winter sky, I left the hotel and ventured in search of food, memories of my first night in Spain siphoning what little ambition I had to explore the area. Not two hundred yards from the hotel, however, I happened upon a menu taped to the inside of a front window, on which I recognized spagety and not much else. Next to the menu hung a sign on a hook, the kind that can be flipped Open/Closed, but, not knowing the words for open or closed in Czech, I was forced to make binoculars with my hands and lean into the tinted windows, startling a chef and a waitress standing by the bar. I yanked open the door and felt a draft of warm air assault my face.

I pointed to a table. "Yes? It's okay?"

The waitress was blond. She smiled and shook her head. Private party. Go away.

Giving up, I trekked back to the hotel, shoved a few koruna in the vending machines and watched CNN International while wolfing a dinner of Kit-Kat-imitation chocolate bars and several bags of salt and vinegar chips. Junk food in a hotel room wasn't as bad as getting lost wandering the streets of Gijon, but I still had some work to do mastering my first meal in a new place.

Early one morning a few days later, two full days into my tryout, our mammoth team bus lumbered away from Liberec, sloping southeast towards the city of Ostrava. Ostrava is Prague's little brother when it comes to commerce and culture, and was where I'd play my first game with the Kondori.

A few hours into the drive, black smoke began billowing up the aisle. The engine was on fire. The driver skittered off the road and everyone clamored out, hustling upwind. Someone pulled out a fire extinguisher and managed to kill the flames, but the engine was beyond repair. A replacement bus arrived two hours later, and we filed back on, rested our heads on our balled-up sweatshirts and tried to get some rest.

We arrived in Ostrava twenty minutes before tip-off. Hurriedly, we changed into our uniforms and then charged out onto the court for an abbreviated warm-up. I had barely shot a single layup when I realized I had to use the bathroom. Urgently. I clenched like a Soviet fist and darted off the court and into the arena's back hallways in search of a toilet. I didn't want to use the locker room because I didn't want the coaches to see me not warming up. I didn't want to blow up one of the public restrooms either, the ones by the main entrance, because it wasn't exactly the time or place for a meet-and-greet with fans. After some maze-like movements, trying doors at random, descending and ascending stairways like in a video game, I somehow found a little bathroom next to what looked like a janitor's closet, though it was immediately apparent that said janitor was either neglectful or forgetful about cleaning his own bathroom. The water in the bowl was a feverish brown hue and smelled like a crusty microwave. I reached for some toilet paper. There was none.

Minutes before I was due to debut my Czech half-season, and my second swing at a professional basketball career, I was not out warming up with my teammates but alone in some filthy bathroom stall, debating my shitting standards, which in this case meant considering whether or not I was okay shitting without toilet paper. I wasn't thinking about the few set plays I'd learned in the scattering of practices I'd been a part of so far, nor did I mentally rehearse the scouting reports on our opponent's big men, how we'd defend the pick-n-roll, or whether we'd double their center.

In hindsight and however disgusting, this ill-timed excreta was actually rather felicitous. The smoky bus too, for that matter. These two interruptions shook up my routine, twisted my brain a little and kept me from fretting about the contract implications this game would have. If I played poorly I'd likely fail my tryout, after which Mike, for all his cache as an agent, would struggle to land me a job in third-division Lichtenstein.

I didn't start the game, instead checking in somewhere

towards the end of the first quarter. It was my first real game in a month and a half, and my first with meaningful minutes in much longer. I felt fine, played decently, but for my first few minutes on the court I was more potential than kinetic with my energy. Then, towards the end of the second quarter, I nailed a three from the corner, right in front of our bench, after which a teammate smacked my ass and in Czech-accented English yelled, "Yahh!" as I ran back on defense. I could hear my other teammates cheering, and the sequence bumped my personal aplomb up over some critical mass, and I went into the locker room at halftime feeling invigorated.

In the second half I scored 21 points as we handed Ostrava their first home loss of the season. I finished with 26 for the game, but the stat guys messed up and gave me 28, and I hadn't scored 28 points in a game, mistakenly or not, since high school. The 28 points effectively ended my tryout, and Dalek moved to sign me for the rest of the year. Mike, doing his part, moved to make sure I received everything I'd been promised (Dalek, ominously, had been maneuvering to cheapen the original agreement). Within a few days the particulars were all worked out, and I signed through the season with Kondori Liberec BC. I gave Dalek my bank information, and he promised me he would wire the first installment of my salary pronto.

My second game with the Condors was the following week. It was also an away game, though in a less hostile arena. Our opponent's fans weren't as vicious as Ostrava's, more of the politely-applauding tennis or golf variety. We arrived a couple hours before tip-off — no fiery engines en route — and with plenty of time to warm-up and take all the shits I needed in stalls that were well stocked with high-ply toilet paper.

In 1951, Junius Kellogg, a center for Manhattan College, was offered $1,000 to shave points in a forthcoming game against DePaul. Kellogg refused and informed his coach, who informed the school president, who informed the New York district attorney, who ultimately implicated dozens of players at seven schools in a massive point-shaving scandal that eventually reached the highest echelons of college basketball. Among those implicated were City College of New York, which in 1950 had won both the NCAA tournament and the NIT, the only team in history to pull off such a feat. Also fingered was the powerhouse that was the Kentucky Wildcats, coached by Adolph Rupp. The Wildcats were forced to sit out the entire 1952-53 season as a result. Much of the ordeal was likely orchestrated by Kentucky bookie Ed Curd, who was good friends with Rupp and who was similarly close with New York City crime boss Frankie Costello, head of the Luciano clan, one of the city's five mob families. Curd is a legend, having introduced to the gambling world both the point spread and the vigorish, two innovations that forever altered the way gamblers place wagers.

Point-shaving is in essence a form of sabotage, an act of deliberately performing under one's ability to avoid meeting an expectation. While point-shaving is a conscious event, usually engineered by an external force, many other variants of sabotage are made manifest totally within the head of the saboteur. Consider the athlete who refuses to try his hardest in order to avoid having to directly face failure should he lose. In the event of a likely defeat, he can tell himself he lost because he didn't try, which is an explanation easier on the ego than having given all that he had and still coming up short.

In my second game in the Czech Republic, I had 4 lethargic points in an unexpected loss, a performance made worse by all-too-familiar strains of self-paralysis reappearing like sky-darkening clouds through the cracks of my consciousness.

"The main thing I have to prevent myself from becoming is disillusioned with transitory success," Bill Bradley, the Princeton star who spent his first professional season in Italy, said while still in college in the midst of his spectacular senior season. "It's dangerous. It's like a heavy rainstorm. It can do damage or it can do good, permitting something to grow."

I had scored 28 points in the league's toughest arena one night, then clocked a ho-hum, head-clenchingly mediocre 4 points four days later against a lesser, middling team. On the bus ride home I ruminated on the explanation I'd quickly identified as the cause of the shift: self-concept. The expectations I'd created with that first game were unsustainable, as I did not, at some critical subconscious level, see myself as a ferociously talented professional athlete who could consistently drop 25 points a game, even if I was perfectly capable of doing so. After my 4-point outing, I was averaging 16 points a game, a much more self-congruent figure. Put another way, I wasn't disillusioned by my transitory success — I was scared of it, and so I'd self-sabotaged until I felt comfortable again. Whatever the cause of my lackluster performance, basketball is won by stats but determined by story.

There was no meal-a-day perk worked into my Czech contract like there'd been in Gijon, but I still ate daily at La Fonduta, the restaurant by the hotel where the blond waitress had shooed me away on New Year's Eve. Her name was Adela, and she was amusingly patient as I figured out the Czech menu. The first time I tried to order sparkling water, I made a drinking motion and then a sizzling sound like steaks on a grill. She looked at me funny and brought me a Coke. But I soon figured out where to point on the menu, and Adela eventually figured out my gestures for water and more bread, and in time we developed a little rapport. She taught me how to say hello in Czech, and I taught her to say "What's up, Ian?"

A couple weeks into my stay in Liberec, Dalek suggested I forget La Fonduta for a night and invited me to his house for dinner. Dalek was in the minority of Czechs who didn't drink alcohol, but still, being Czech, he drank non-alcoholic beer, which he served me my own bottle of as I sat down at the kitchen table inside his modest home. His wife stood by the stove, hovering over simmering pots and pans.

"You like the beer here?" Dalek asked me as we clinked bottles and swigged. The Czech Republic, I would come to know, has the highest per capita beer consumption rate in the world. The Czechs, in fact, drink so much beer they've built about a thousand "non-stops" (this is actually what they're called in Czech, "non-stops"), small huts sprinkled across the country like gas stations that serve cheap beer and hard spirits and savory snacks twenty four-seven. Not quite a bar but not really a grocery store, the non-stops basically serve to ensure that on Czech soil there are no such things as alcohol deserts.

I had drunk a good amount of Czech beer since my arrival, and I indeed heartily approved, but I also knew Dalek worked no-alcohol clauses into his contracts, including mine. "Standard procedure for all our players," he told me when he'd pointed it out.

So I was aware of the clause, as was Dalek, which fashioned his inquiry into a sort of trick question.

He cut in before I could answer. "I love beer. I drink it after workouts. Good B vitamins. Great for recovery." However many years or decades ago, Dalek said, the Czech government realized that Czech citizens were drinking so much beer that even poor people's meager wages were often being spent on drink instead of food. To ensure the country was getting essential nutrition, the government coerced beer manufacturers to fortify their product with whatever vitamins and minerals they could squeeze in.

Dalek's wife set three hot plates on the table, chunks of steaming potato and drippy pork and a salad of pickled cabbage and carrots — classic Eastern European fare. She briefly sat down before jumping back up, taking her plate with her, off to tend to some unseen matter, and leaving Dalek and me alone in the kitchen. Dalek began attacking his meal with an intensity that only a man who takes himself very seriously can pull off. His seriousness, I decided, was the byproduct of being the kind of guy who couldn't quite believe the job he'd lucked into. An engineer of some sort by training, he didn't have much of a basketball pedigree. It felt like he was perpetually surprised that he was in charge, and to mask that surprise he'd mastered the stone face, because of course everybody knows that pro basketball is nothing if not serious. He never really turned his business-mode off either, which meant our dinner would be nothing more than an extended tryout, even though I'd already signed.

Dalek interrupted his chewing to ask why I played.

"You mean like, basketball?" I said.

Dalek smiled the way serious people smile, close-lipped and sour-eyed.

In retrospect I can appreciate the foregoing of small talk, but the abruptness of the question at the time was jarring.

"Basketball," Dalek said, expanding his query. "Why do you think you compete?"

I took a sip of my beer and hurriedly rehearsed potential responses. If I'd known Dalek a little better, I might've responded:

Well gee, Dalek, that's a great question. I'll take a stab at it, why not. So, why do I play? Why do I compete? Well, my dad's tall, and my mom's not short, and my grandfather was 6'6" back in the days when being 6'6" was like a crane, so I have the height. I played other sports growing up too, notably soccer, and I actually liked soccer as much as basketball for a while, but then in eighth grade I got cut from my travel soccer team, which I took pretty hard. That same year I averaged 30-some points a game in a competitive local YMCA basketball league, and I got a little more crane-like myself and started playing some decent AAU ball. So things were kind of falling into place, and by the time I reached high school it was pretty much a given I'd try out for the team, because that's what tall people with potential do — am I right Dalek? They try to *make it*. Anyway, I made Junior Varsity and played really well, and by the end of the year people were talking about my promising future on Varsity. They said I could play in college, maybe on scholarship. At the time basketball was mostly fun, Dalek. I liked being good at it and loved the moments when I could just play. It made me anxious, but not *that* kind of anxious. I had these weird superstitions,

83

you might call them symptoms, that were kind of odd when I thought about them, but everybody had superstitions. I didn't think about why I played; there was no need. It would've been like asking a kid at the playground why he's having fun.

My sophomore year, Dalek, I started getting letters from colleges, early pitches from coaches who'd eventually offer me four-year scholarships worth six figures to come play at their schools. After my junior season, my AAU coach thought it would be a good idea if I left Charlottesville to play my senior year for Oak Hill Academy, some boarding school I'd never heard of in bodunk, Virginia. I ended up going, Dalek, pretty much exclusively for basketball reasons, and if I'm leaving home before I really have to, if I'm giving up my senior year at home for basketball's sake, I guess that means I'm pretty invested in the game. Anyway, I committed to play college ball at Davidson, and man, Dalek, once you're playing Division I, that's pretty much your life. Suddenly your whole existence revolves around hooping, if it didn't already before. And then you play decently in college and people start talking about pro ball, maybe not the NBA, but you're definitely good enough to play in some high-level European leagues.

People keep telling you you can make it overseas, though you're still not sure what *making it* means, as the definition is perpetually tied to an ambiguous achievement that is continuously bumped further and further into the future. Making it is only a carrot, you realize. It's like you play growing up only to make the high school team, and then you play high school only to get to college, and then you play college only to get to the pros, and you play well in the pros only to earn your next contract, and so on. Part of you questions why you want to keep playing after college, but what other option is there? It's not like you can see yourself in finance or dentistry or something mundane like that, and besides, you're still pretty raw when it comes to making decisions for yourself.

It sucks, Dalek, because the more you keep investing, the more you have to keep playing to keep validating that additional investment. I mean, think about it, if you gave up a "regular" college experience — the kind of sport-free college experience that years later, when you reflect, you sometimes wish you had — then you'd probably go to some lengths to make that sacrifice worth it. Plus, who quits a lifelong pursuit right when he's about to start making money from it? Are you starting to see, Dalek, why I play and compete? Let's say you were me. If you gave up basketball, what would you do? What exactly is your skill set otherwise? Do you have any idea? You can't honestly tell me you have any clue about yourself away from the game. You play basketball, that's what you know how to do, and so you keep playing it. The sport is you and you are the sport. This type of reversible sentence is called a chiasmus, which you might have learned in the advanced English classes you never took in college because you felt so bogged down with balling. Sure, often basketball's not fun. Often it makes you super-anxious, and yes, *that* kind of anxious, but you don't know anything else; basketball has become you, and you have become basketball. The bounce of a ball and the resounding echo in an empty gym, the echo extra loud in the shell of your life that you hope won't be as empty once you walk off the court. That's your meditative gong: the bounce and the echo. The cheers from fans when you score, the approval of coaches, and high fives from teammates, these are the fuels that feed your self-worth. Your name stitched across the back of your jersey is your identity, and your stat line is your Social Security number. Walk away from this and you have no idea who you are. So you keep playing. You *have* to keep playing, and the longer you stay in the game the harder it is to see yourself as anything other than a Basketball Player, so you stay in the game to stay who you are.

That's not to say I wouldn't do it all again if I could. I'm not saying that at all, because there are some really incredible angles of basketball that I'm pretty grateful to be a part of, but it's just that you asked.

Does that answer your question, Dalek?

There was an irritable feeling in my stomach as I scrambled to come up with an actual answer. I coughed and took another swig of my beer. "I think I play for fun. Because it's fun. I like the camaraderie I feel with my teammates," I said. This was at least half true, half of the time.

"I play to win," Dalek responded immediately, as if I hadn't responded, as if the whole point of the question had been to set up his answer to it.

Dalek's expression betrayed hints of self-satisfaction, his nostrils flaring a little wider and his eyes slitting a little thinner, ever closer to that elusive sneeze.

"Yeah," I said, feeling stupid that I'd stooped to answer the question with his approval in mind. "Yeah, I get that."

Before I left Dalek's house, I asked him whether he'd wired my salary. He said he had and that it should arrive in my account before the end of the week.

I wasn't the only one on the team who enjoyed getting my vitamins and minerals from Czech beer, nor the only one willing to risk violating the no-alcohol clause to do so. On nights out our team frequented our own little speakeasy of sorts, the Sailor Pub, a place with golden anchors and nautical maps on the walls, located in a darker part of the city. We sat around thick medieval-ish wooden tables emptying fifty-cent pints, and when enough glasses were empty somehow an accordion would materialize and it'd be time to sing Czech folk tunes. Whenever the Czech guys were good and hoarse and whenever I started to believe I knew the words, we'd squeeze into taxis and zip over to the legendary Zanzibar, the bar attached to the local university, where seemingly every Liberecian under the age of thirty-five hung out on Friday and Saturday nights. I was much freer in the Czech Republic than I'd been in Spain, less attached to expectations and outcomes, and as a result, I was less encumbered by my obsessive-compulsive symptoms, which seemed more like annoying chores to check off than anything seriously debilitating.

My mind, therefore, had a lot more free space, and it was in Liberec that I first did some serious writing, producing in the span of several months a novella. The protagonist was a twenty-something party-loving male studying abroad in Europe. One night while he's out drinking he meets a beautiful and enigmatic woman who, a half-hour into their conversation, tells him she's a pseudo-alien, part of a colony of former Earthlings who fled the solar system long ago for political reasons (the geopolitical inter-planetary situation is complicated). She's visiting Earth in search of a suitable sperm donor, as all the men on her home planet are irreversibly infertile.

The alien's name is Adela, which was, of course, the name of the blonde waitress at La Fonduta, and the name of my novella was, eponymously, heroically, *Duty for Adela*. Adela (the real one) was around my age, was playful in a mischievous kind of way, and had eyes that always made her seem like she was thinking about something a little sad. She did her part to uphold the Czech Republic's high aesthetic standard when it comes to women, and, unless she and I revved up our language tutoring, was eternally mysterious, a trait which only increased her allure and added to the speculation with which I molded her fictitiously into my pages.

The novella's protagonist falls madly in love with Adela, and if you possess anything resembling a functional nervous system you can probably draw some parallels between how the protagonist feels about the fictitious Adela and how I felt about the real Adela who brought me my meal every day. Our interactions at the restaurant were almost narcotic, carbonated with that covetous thrill that accompanies impossibility. I wanted her, but everything we did was likewise tinged with a gnawing sense that our mutual attraction might not be so mutual after all, that she might be a tease and was simply having a little fun with the massively tall American who lumbered in everyday. The way Adela's hand may or may not have brushed my shoulder as she set down my plate. The way we may or may not have locked gazes an extra second longer than we needed to. The way we flirtatiously dropped a word of the other's language into our non-conversations. I liked how indecipherable she was, yet the possibility of a "real" relationship remained impractical, and, in a way, undesired, as I'm not sure we would've gotten along had we been able to converse in a non-sublexical language.

But, alas, it didn't matter, as Adela was involved in a sugar-daddy capacity with some businessman at least twice her age, a guy with a fluffed pillow for a stomach who I'd see at the restaurant every couple of weeks, at which times Adela's smile would flatten and she'd suddenly become very serious, even pouty, and ignore my table.

By March, two full months into my contract, my bank account still looked like the front fender of an Audi. I spent a lot of my interactions with Dalek formulating different ways of asking him the same thing, and Dalek kept telling me he'd sent the money. Mike told me to ask Dalek for a bank receipt, but when I did so he told me he must've been mistaken and that the money actually hadn't yet been sent. Apologetically, he told me not to worry and that he would send the money immediately.

Meanwhile, on the court, we were cranking out wins and fighting up rungs in the league standings. We were now squarely in a playoff spot, in line with the team's preseason goals, and the question turned to whether or not we could pull off an upset and advance past the first round.

In 1964, the NBA turned eighteen, and, like many teenagers, the league at the time was struggling to make its way in the world. Ask the average American of the era his or her favorite sport, and you would likely have heard football, baseball, boxing, horse racing and who knows what else before NBA Basketball jumped on the list.

The '64 All-Star game in Boston, Massachusetts, however, was a chance for the league to show off its rising stock of stars — Elgin Baylor, Wilt Chamberlain, Bill Russell, Jerry West and Oscar Robertson, among others, were in their primes — an opportunity created when ABC agreed to broadcast the event, the first NBA All-Star game to be shown live on national television. Thousands of fans excitedly packed the seats of the Boston Garden, eyeballing the camera crews setting up their equipment, and many thousands more were tuning in on their television sets at home, a good segment of them new to the sport and curious to see what this uniquely American game had to offer in the way of mass entertainment.

The stage was set, the equipment was functioning, and the fans were juiced, but in the hours before the game a discouraging rumor quietly began spreading among the operating staff: there might not be any players available to take the floor. Boston legend Tommy Heinsohn, then just a year away from retirement, was both a member of the East squad and the president of the Players Association. As the league's stars made their way through blizzard conditions to Boston — with most arriving the day of the game — he met them each at the hotel and encouraged them to sign a sheet of paper. The paper was a written commitment not to play the game unless the league's front office met a specific list of demands. No matter how exciting and marketable the league's stars had become, in 1964 those stars still hadn't earned a seat at the proverbial table, and, with the NBA turning eighteen, it was perhaps fitting (and overdue) that the players were demanding the right to vote. "The players were controlled by the owners," L.A. Laker legend Jerry West told the *Los Angeles Times* in 2011 of the situation. "All of us felt like we were slaves in the sense we had no rights. No one made anything then. You had to work in the summer. It was the stone ages of basketball."

Indeed, Heinsohn was the president of the Players Association primarily because he worked for an insurance company in the offseason, and therefore knew a little more about numbers. The Players Association, despite being founded ten years earlier in 1954 by Bob Cousy (making it the oldest trade union of the four major North American sports), still wasn't officially recognized by the league, and the players, fed up, felt they had no choice but to strike. They wanted a reworked pension plan, better training staffs, and more consideration regarding the schedule. It wasn't unusual, for example, for a team to play a game Saturday night and then another game Sunday afternoon. The owners had for months repeatedly promised the players they'd hear their concerns, but had ignored or stood up the players whenever an opportunity to talk arose, and even on the day of the All-Star game itself, when the NBA's board of governors had met, they'd refused to invite anyone from the Players Association to the meeting.

Enough was enough, and the All-Star game boycott materialized. According to Heinsohn, the owners were made aware around 5 p.m., just hours before tip-off, that no player would take the floor unless their demands were met. The owners gathered outside the locker room furiously pleading and making threats, but the players wouldn't budge. They stayed cooped up in the locker room, an Irish cop guarding the door, while the game clock ticked off the minutes until start time. Meanwhile, the capacity crowd was starting to wonder why nobody was warming up, and ABC, which had gotten word of the situation, was threatening the cancel the game altogether if the players didn't materialize, potentially a tremendous embarrassment and a huge blow to the credibility of the league. Finally, after much heated and rushed debate among the owners, J. Walter Kennedy, the commissioner, asked to enter the locker room. He stood before the group of All-Stars and declared that the league office would formally recognize the Players Association, and that the owners would meet each one of their demands, but they would have to hustle out and play the game, which, by some accounts, was already delayed. Without much in the way of warm-up, the players stitched together four exciting quarters, with the East edging the West 111-107 behind 26 points from Oscar Robertson. All publicity disasters were averted. Postgame footage shows the commissioner handing a content-looking Robertson the MVP trophy, a symbolic gesture of the growth of player power to come.

If the Czech league had a players association, I didn't know about it, and by April, all on my own, I was threatening to sit out if I didn't get paid. Or rather Mike was telling me this was a last resort, sitting out, but a viable and increasingly necessary last resort, as my money was still M.I.A. I relayed to both Coach Ales and Dalek my considerations about not playing. I tried to be nice about it, as I didn't want Ales cutting my playing time over bad feelings in case the money suddenly came through, and I didn't want Dalek thinking I was trying to fight him for the money and give him any excuse not to send it. Both Ales and Dalek gave me legitimate-sounding reasons why the money hadn't been sent. A change of ownership, different banks, different accounts. "It's not just you," they said, "none of the players are getting anything." This might've been true, but as the only foreigner on the team I was operating under a different set of circumstances.

By this point I didn't know what or who to believe, and I was having trouble caring. Living expenses in the Czech Republic were comparatively cheap and I still had money from Spain. Most of the worst of my obsessive-compulsive symptoms were still on hiatus. I was getting along well with my teammates, playing decently, and was generally enjoying my time in the country.

Money, in a way, felt like a bonus, but still, money mattered, especially when I found out certain guys on the team *had* been paid portions of their salaries in January and February. A few games before the playoffs I gave the team my ultimatum. They had one week to put a minimum of two months salary into my bank account or I'd refuse to play until they did.

Dalek and I met in his office to try and talk it out. When he realized I wasn't going to budge, he said to give him a few minutes, and with me sitting right there he proceeded to make a series of phone calls, cashing in favors, scraping the dry bottoms of the team's bank accounts, trying to scrounge up what cash he could. After each phone call he jotted a figure on a Post-it note. On more than one occasion he ran a hand back through his hair, his eyes wide, inhaling sharply, as if the person on the other end had revealed something horrid. After ten minutes he hung up the phone a final time, added the figures, and quoted me a number down to the cent. "I can get you this much," he said. It was a little under half of a month's salary. I stared back at him as if through a glass wall. I'd given him the benefit of the doubt for months, but eventually the truth was too bright to ignore, and now his credibility was no longer even worth the arbitrary number he'd quoted me. I don't think he even made a single call; it was a show. He'd been speaking to a dial tone for those ten minutes, wanting to seem desperate, like he was doing all he could, like I was somehow being greedy, like I was somehow siphoning the nutrients from his precious non-alcoholic beer. Maybe he *had* done all he could, maybe he really *was* making desperate phone calls on my behalf, but that wasn't my perception from across the office then, and I still hold that same perception now, and I guess there's no way of knowing. I shook my head at the Post-it note and felt horrible.

I didn't wait the full week. That afternoon, after getting the coach to sign a handwritten note stating that he understood my decision and agreed with it, I showed up for practice but not to practice. I sat on the bench, immobile but sweating, feeling lame and caged, my mind analyzing the situation from all possible points of view — my own, the team's, my teammates', the fans', legal, moral, ethical – to determine which point of view was correct, and to determine whether I had real rationale in sitting out or whether I was being some eggheaded American.

For their part, my Czech teammates didn't give me any shaming looks. They treated me the way participating practice players might treat an injured player, indifferently and kind of dismissively, but not degradingly. They weren't getting paid either, but as domestic players they didn't have the luxury of holding out. Again, I was the only foreigner; I had to navigate on my own. Towards the end of practice one of our guards subbed out and came and sat by me on the bench. He grabbed a dry-erase clipboard and wrote Kondori, then morphed the "r" and the "i" into an "m." He smiled slightly, tossed me the clipboard and hustled back on the court.

Mike eventually pulled together half of all that I was owed, but not until June, and not until long after I'd said goodbye to Liberec and to Adela, to Coach and to the guys on the team. Not until I'd left Liberec in mid-April, a few days before the playoffs I'd helped us make, and not until I'd packed up my still half-empty suitcase and zoomed back down the E-65, sitting next to a chauffeuring Dalek, both of us pretending like nothing was amiss.

One afternoon, back in Liberec, a couple weeks before I left, I was the only patron in La Fonduta. Adela was waitressing, wearing a black apron and a purple shirt. Sometimes the shirt would ride up a little and I could see a sliver of tattoo just over the rim of her jeans. Throughout my meal we had one of our non-conversations, a goofy borderline-awkward kind of exchange, the kind of infatuation-laced schoolyard banter you cringe at when you're witnessing it as a third party, but which is really sort of wonderful and riveting when you're a participant. Especially when you're still an amorously-inclined twenty-two year old and hanging out with the woman who over the past couple months has inspired you to write a lengthy and leading-lady-reverent piece of fiction.

As I rose to leave I walked past Adela at the bar. For the moment we were the only two people in the restaurant. I was quite obviously stalling, soaking up our aloneness, and she was giving me reason to stall, and for a few seconds or so we grinned stupidly at each other. Adela looked around, and then she looked at me. Her grin increased in radiance until it reached a wattage that could only signify a certain kind of long-awaited suggestion or invitation, and my brain immediately and furiously tried to confirm that it was picking up the right signals. When I was able to pull myself together, I stooped and slid my hands around Adela's waist as she tilted back and reached up her arms to encircle my neck. Later that evening I added another word to my list of Czech vocabulary: polibek.

The ending of my novella is inevitable. The protagonist and Adela are from different parts of the galaxy. On the last page there's a cloaked spaceship in low orbit, lazily circling Earth, waiting to whisk her at high speeds back to her home planet, alone.

Chapter 5 — Addiction Part Two

A couple months later, in late September 2007, I flew to Sweden on a two-month tryout to play for the Norrkoping Dolphins, a team situated a few hours drive south of Stockholm. In the locker room before my first practice, I found the only available cubby, one quite recently vacated, as Norrkoping had, two days prior, cut another American after he'd failed his own tryout. The guy's name was written in masking tape above my locker which I immediately ripped off, wondering if my status on the team was just as precarious.

I wasn't supposed to be in Sweden. The previous spring, following my early departure from the Czech Republic, I could be found breathing exhaust in the bed of a muffler-troubled pickup in Cofradia, a small town in northwestern Honduras, where I was visiting friends from college who taught at a local bilingual school. It was still early in the day, but the sun was already reddening my sun-starved arms, which were gripped to the truck as we bounced along the uneven dirt roads like vegetables shaken in a wok. I was trying hard not to think about basketball, but I'd been tagged by my Davidson friends to guest-teach PE, and there was really only one subject that I wanted on my syllabus.

I was given domain over the dirt field out back behind the school, a space about the size of a baseball diamond. I'd brought a few basketballs with me from Charlottesville, which were tucked under my arms as I watched my charges file out of the open-air school building for a little exercise with Mr Ee-yann, as I was soon rechristened.

"Basquetbol," I said, holding up one of the balls. "Vamos a jugar basquetbol."

"What's basketball?" a few of them asked, before wondering aloud why we weren't going to play fútbol.

Largely as a byproduct of the Industrial Revolution and its concomitant inflow of cash, an increasing swath of American citizens in the 1800s were not only leading more sedentary lifestyles (particularly white citizens in the South) but also finding themselves with an influx of free time. Free time was a novel commodity for most Americans, and it created a vexing question previously unavailable to the average citizen, namely, *what to do*? The leisure of choice, predictably, was often vice, and many Americans chose to spend their surplus hours enjoying a round at the bar or a romp at the brothel. These activities aroused no shortage of concern in the minds of America's more pious individuals, who thought that all the extra free time would be better spent serving God. In both adolescent America and old world Europe, missionaries ramped up their efforts to instill both physical and spiritual sanity in the average American. Among this wave of cultural evangelists was George Williams, a draper's apprentice who in London, England in 1844 founded the first YMCA with the purpose of "improving the spiritual condition of young men engaged in the drapery, embroidery, and other trades."

Williams' moralizing movement quickly expanded away from Anglo window trappings and soon crossed the ocean, and by the late 19th-century hundreds of YMCAs dotted the American landscape, particularly in New England, including in Springfield, Massachusetts where in 1891 the International YMCA Training Center included among its faculty a twenty-nine year old Canadian named James Naismith.

Naismith was representative of what was then known as muscular Christianity, a movement that, like the YMCA, traces its origins to a multifarious America transitioning out of the Industrial Revolution. Its promoters espoused the exigency of athletics and manliness, hoping to purge from young men "all that is effeminate, un-English, and excessively intellectual." Naismith, a deeply pious man from Ontario — we'd call him "straight edge" in today's parlance — was influenced by this philosophy, and gave up a career in the ministry in hopes of finding a way to somehow merge athletics with God through physical education, an intention that sparked his migration south to the United States. Today, PE degrees can be earned in big cities in Asia and small towns in Honduras, but in 1891 the only school in North America to offer a degree in PE was the YMCA Training Center in Springfield, which would, after the arrival of Naismith, soon add a much more eternal distinction to its heritage: the birthplace of basketball.

From a big-picture perspective, basketball grew out of a rivulet of cultural upshots running through the 19th century — a post-Industrial Revolution response to a boon of middle-class wealth and free time — but if you zoom in to the Training Center's director's office in Springfield in December 1891, you'd discover that the more temporal impetus for Naismith's invention was the moment when that director, one Dr. Gulick, asked Naismith to come up with a team game that could safely be played indoors in cold months under "artificial light." After days of fretting and a few mistrials, Naismith came up with basket-ball, and basketball instantly went the 1890s version of viral.

There are basketball deists who like to claim that Naismith conjured the game out of nothing the way Elohim on Day One summoned light, but, in truth, in conceiving basketball Naismith was as much an interpreter as he was an inventor, drawing from the sports he already knew and rearranging their parts to fit the circumstances.

Team sports in 1891, Naismith mused, like tennis and football and baseball, had balls, so Naismith determined his game should also have a ball. Naismith wanted his new game to be safer than football, so he legislated against tackling by prohibiting players from running with the ball. Finally, he plucked from a kid's game called Duck on a Rock the idea to hang the goals above the grasp of the players.

Drawing on the missionary power and global reach of the YMCA, basketball quickly spread across the world — including Mel Rideout to Montmartre, Paris in 1893 — but 130 years later there were still parts of the world to which basketball was more or less a stranger, like Cofradia, Honduras in 2007. It was a source of both pride and frustration for me that none of my PE students at the bilingual school knew much about the sport that ran my life. Pride because I knew the game and could teach them to play, and frustration because I wanted everyone in the world to love basketball, particularly all these adoring little kids, as if their love would somehow substantiate my unflinching dedication to the game.

Wiping sweat from my forehead every few minutes, I

channeled Naismith and attempted to explain a few basic concepts to the students. It was harder than I imagined, teaching basketball, as I'd never taught the game from scratch before, particularly not in a foreign language to a group of restless kids. Yet explaining the game seemed exceptionally simple: put the ball in the basket, and don't let the other team do the same.

After my simplified introduction I passed out the balls and put the kids in small groups to explore, but the sunbaked field's random mounds and craters made dribbling difficult. Since there was no hoop to practice shooting I made a circle with my arms, like I was hugging a ghost, at which point the kids would run up and slam the ball home. Not quite understanding what was going on, the kids squealed with delight, squeals that would disappear later in the week when I capitulated to popular demand and brought out the soccer balls. Suddenly, the kids were ultra-serious, imitating on that ratty little field the supposed swagger and gravitas of the international superstars they adored from afar. The breezy fun of our basketball sessions disappeared, replaced by a kind of worried tension. To them, basketball was jovial and untroubled, and could be fully enjoyed in the capacity of the kids they were. Conversely, they played fútbol with the heavy weight of culture and expectation on their shoulders. I understood the shift.

In late July of that same summer, at a time on the calendar when teams that are still looking to sign foreigners are moving on to their latter choices, I heard from Kouvola Basket, a Finnish team. The deal I was offered was decent enough, but it came with a caveat: I'd start the season on a two-week tryout, like in Liberec.

"It's just a formality," Mike told me over the phone when he called to talk things over. "They do it with everybody. They just want to make sure you're not some deadbeat."

"Sounds good to me," I replied, and in August of 2007 I packed up my gear and flew to Kouvola, Finland to begin my second professional season in Europe. Kouvola was grey, perhaps bleak, but simultaneously clean and pleasant in a resigned kind of way. After two weeks of practices and scrimmages in which I performed remarkably average, the GM asked me to lunch with him at a restaurant downtown, where we picked nonchalantly at our food, making small talk and avoiding eye contact. The very moment the waiter came and set the bill down, the GM looked at me and, in a voice already leaking pity, said, "Vee have decided nut to keep your contract."

I nodded and pretended like I understood his reasoning, without actually having heard it. The waiter, the scene's indelicate testimonial witness, nosily studied both our faces before retreating. I wanted to retreat, too, but there was nowhere to go.

The luncheon was more awkward and unsettling than it should've been, as the two-week tryout really might've been a formality. Those first couple weeks had seen the team set me up with an apartment, a cell phone, and a Finnish bank account, and the team had even leased me a car. I thought I'd played well.

From the restaurant the GM and I drove straight to the bank, where after wiring two-weeks pay back to the States I closed the account I had just recently opened. Then I drove in my soon-to-be returned car to my soon-to-be-vacated apartment, where I packed up my things and contemplated quitting basketball. My love of the game, if I had any love left, was missing in action. Perhaps the GM sensed this, even before he cut me.

"A team in Sweden is looking for a big guy," Mike said when he reached me two weeks later in Germany, where I was staying with a former Davidson teammate. The Swedish deal wasn't great financially and I would again be forced into a tryout, this time lasting two months, but it wasn't like I could've held out for something better. I silently sighed and aloud said "sure I'll take it, when do I leave?"

Not caring about anything anymore, I scored 30 points on the road in Norrkoping's season opener, a career high, more than I'd ever scored in college or even high school.

In the locker room after the game I noticed one of my new teammates staring at me curiously. "Why aren't you more excited?" he asked. "You just dropped *thirty*."

I blinked at him, not knowing what to say, not wanting to share what I feared was going to come next: a bad game to balance out the good, like had happened in Liberec and at Davidson. My issue with basketball wasn't a question of scaling the requisite cliffs, it was a matter of staying on top long enough to call myself consistent. When I cared about my success, I had yet to learn how to healthily deal with it, and I was afraid of it for any number of obscure reasons.

During my second game in Sweden, near the end of the first quarter, I missed an easy layup, the kind that causes the crowd to collectively inhale. Another time I caught the ball and froze, and stood there, literally paralyzed by indecision, until the ref called a five-second violation. My teammates were open — I saw them and knew how to pass them the ball — I just couldn't figure out how to make it happen. By halftime I had just 4 points.

In the locker room during the break, I grabbed a cup of Red Bull and sat down at my cubby, which still didn't feature a permanent placard above it that said "Johnson." There was no name above it at all, not even on a torn strip of masking tape.

As we waited for the coaches to come in, I stared into my cup and heard myself tell myself, *Just don't give a fuck.* This had been the unsolicited advice given to me some days earlier by the former Davidson teammate I'd stayed with in Germany. I repeated it now again and again, its clarity increasing with every repetition. It was a mental state predicated on the inverse of what most coaches had been telling me for years, that the more I cared, the farther I'd go. Perhaps this was true, but in some cases the less you give a fuck, the more freedom you acquire.

Dallas Mavericks great Dirk Nowitzki once let slip that when he shoots free throws he'll often sing or hum the tune to *Baywatch*, the idea being that if he's singing, he's not getting distracted by negative thoughts. In that regard, it's also possible that my *Just don't give a fuck* phrasing acted as a kind of mental screen. If a mantra was occupying my thoughts, other, more paralyzing thoughts, were kept at bay. Maybe I could've said, "two tablespoons of lemon juice," and achieved the same effect.

Whatever the underlying reasons, the phrasing undoubtedly helped. I finished that second game with 24 points in a commanding win and proceeded to string together a series of great performances. I set a new career high with 36 points one game, then soon after scored 39, then a couple games later dropped another 39 in just 24 minutes. In acknowledgment, Norrkoping picked up my contract for the rest of the year.

My monthly payments arrived on time, which any European player will tell you is as good an indicator as any as to the professionalism of the club, but my payments, however, weren't exactly breaking anybody's bank. When Norrkoping signed me, I wasn't quite a charity case, but I was close. After three more or less failed first tries in under a year, the team had no obligation to pay me anything, and I signed for a salary that would turn out to be by far my lowest as a pro. (Relatively speaking, of course; one can speculate how far a single monthly payment in Norrkoping would've gone in a place like Cofradia.) These relatively sparse monthly payments, however, felt like exactly what I deserved. In other words, my salary fit my self-concept, and as a result I didn't have to worry about whether or not I was "earning" the money I was making, and I didn't feel funny or guilty about playing basketball for a living like I did in Spain, because I wasn't making much of one.

In January, Swedish fans voted me to start in that month's All-Star game, held in a sold-out arena in Stockholm. As I stood in the tunnel with my fellow players while some hip-hop artist rapped to the crowd, I was sure that there'd been some mistake, sure that there'd been a miscount or that the fans didn't really know basketball. I was leading the league in scoring at the time, and was top ten in four or five other categories, but if the league's players and coaches had chosen the starters, I told myself, I wouldn't have made it.

By March, we were smack in the middle of the Basketligan

standings, close to securing a playoff spot, while at the same time back home the 2008 NCAA tournament was tipping off. Davidson, led by Stephen Curry, had won the Southern Conference and earned a 10-seed in their bracket. They faced 7-seed Gonzaga in the opening round, where Steph went on to drop 40 points on 14 of 22 shooting in an upset win, after which Davidson became one of the stories of the tournament. Forty-eight hours later, Davidson beat Georgetown in the Round of 32, and then a week after that pulled away from Wisconsin in the Sweet Sixteen, at which point Davidson became *the* story of the tournament.

I followed along from across the Atlantic, but the games were tough to watch because the further Davidson advanced, the more I felt removed from the school. Everything I'd accomplished there was relative, and now, by comparison, practically irrelevant. Just two years removed from campus, I was being demoted to a footnote in the B.C. books of Davidson Basketball — Before Curry. However prideful and self-centered, I could not suppress the shame in knowing that my senior class hadn't made it as far as Curry and his boys, and if we couldn't get there, I felt like no Davidson Wildcat team should. I quietly hated myself for feeling this way, but didn't know how to feel anything else.

In my defense, my mental state was more than pride or self-centeredness. Because I drew my sense of self-worth from the well of my basketball career, Davidson's success without me was, in an indirect way, depleting my sense of self-worth, forcing me to reevaluate the stockpile of memories I could rely on to feel good about myself. So in rooting against Davidson, I was, in a way, rooting for myself.

In 1891, visitors to Coney Island's Old Iron Pier were treated to a novel experience, an "inclined elevator" that mechanically ferried them upwards at a twenty-five degree angle to a waiting platform. Loud and clunky — riders complained of a lack of a moving handrail — it was nonetheless a success, and today there are escalators in almost every major sporting arena, airport, and shopping mall in the world. Its inventor, the New York engineer Jesse W. Reno, patented his device in 1892, and when he sold the patent in 1911 he pocketed enough cash to retire early and live out his days a wealthy man.

1891's other big invention, basketball, would likewise grow to be associated with an increase in height, but James Naismith, unlike Reno, declined to patent his new game, likely costing him an extraordinary amount of income.

Today, money is, of course, the catalyst of all basketball transactions, but the road from Naismith's financial indifference to today's cash-happy NBA has been gradual. The first professional basketball players, back around the turn of the 20th century, were professionals only in that they took home the surplus after gate receipts were doled out to all other expectant palms. Sometimes these early pioneers pocketed a buck, sometimes twenty, although often it was nothing.

As the game's popularity grew, some players were good enough, or well enough connected, to make basketball their only profession. They usually played as part of independent troupes that toured the country performing wherever anyone would hire them to play. (The Original Celtics, the New York Renaissance and the Harlem Globetrotters, three of the most noteworthy teams of the pre-WWII era, spent good portions of their existence independently barnstorming America.) But the money was still iffy and the basketball landscape still chaotic.

In 1925, the American Basketball League was formed. Of the fourteen professional leagues that had preceded it, none had had much staying power, but the ABL introduced what at the time was considered a radical idea — exclusive written contracts — limiting a player to one team and one team only. Gone, then, were the erratic and unpredictable days when players switched teams on a whim, like during the middle of a road trip or even a few minutes before a game, chasing quick dollars wherever they could. The ABL was forced to fold when the Great Depression struck a few years later, but a new and more stable model had nonetheless been forged.

After written contracts, perhaps the next greatest financial impact on the game came via the television. Early on, the major television networks, in scouting the sporting landscape, originally decided that they preferred football. But when television executives realized how lucrative all sports could be, particularly to men, they sought out relationships with athletic leagues wherever they could, including with nascent leagues like the NBA.

Once the NBA partnered with television networks, the major medium of basketball steadily became the pixel, and over time the power of the pixel skyrocketed. In 2018, the average NBA salary was $7.1 million, by far the highest average for any major professional sports league in the world, and this figure is a direct consequence of the 10-year, $24 billion deal the league signed with ABC, ESPN and TNT in 2014.

The NBA, like most sports leagues around the world, is full

of players who would play for $7.10 a game, but who nonetheless, when the opportunity arises, choose to play for the team that offers the most lucrative deal. Team loyalty exists, but is easily usurped by an extra comma. The tears and kisses that stain the Larry O'Brien Trophy every year are signs of real worship, but the championship trophy is just one half of a polytheistic NBA kingdom dually governed by something similarly cold and hard.

I understand the temptation. My season in Norrkoping was by any measure a massive personal success. In addition to starting in the All-Star game, that April both the coaches and media selected me First-Team All-Sweden, having averaged 24 points and 8 rebounds a game for the year. More importantly, I'd played well from the start to the finish of the season, finally eradicating through sheer perseverance and a timely mantra the idea that my triumphs needed to be balanced out by failures of the same degree.

Moving into the offseason, Mike would now answer his phone. The first call that summer came from the Norrkoping front office, offering me a three-year contract extension. The security, familiarity, and my proven success there was enticing, but these were also the very reasons why I was hesitant to accept their offer, as if I felt I didn't deserve those things. I could barely allow myself to play day-to-day, so the thought of signing myself over to a club for three years felt suffocating. Almost immediately after Norrkoping made their offer, Gothia, a team out of Gothenburg, Sweden that had finished in last place the year before, called Mike and offered me a one-year deal for a lot more money. Unlike in previous years, when I more or less had to take the only available offer, I now had a decision to make, and I was trying hard not to make money the only deciding variable.

Chapter 6 — Addiction Part Three

A heavy snow fell against the kitchen window of my apartment in Gothenburg, the condensation splintering the glass, the cold silencing all of nature's instruments, even the wind. Teeth brushed and pajama-clad, I leaned against the window frame, arms crossed, mouth slightly ajar in the way of someone lost in thought. The lights were all off in my apartment, and my silhouette was lit only by street light reflecting off the white carpet, on which footprints had yet to fall.

The previous spring I'd turned down Norrkoping's offer and signed instead with Gothenburg, the west coast squad that had offered me more money. The team had splurged on a few other big names, and our roster was stacked enough for the preseason media to tab us a favorite to win the Basketligan. Our head coach had bragged to anyone who'd listen that we were "so fucking good," but our head coach was also a rookie and had convinced the front office to spend copious amounts of money to sign talent, not chemistry, and so fucking good we were not.

Just a handful of games into the season, our losses had started feel like Civil War reenactments. Everyone showed up dressed and ready to go, but everyone likewise knew the outcome in advance. Any hope of a miraculous transformation was scuttled by an unspoken and collective agreement to give up (there was no relegation in Sweden), at which point everything melted into the kind of frustrated boredom you feel when you check the map and realize you still have hundreds of miles to go, but nothing left to do other than tap the accelerator and keep a lazy hand on the wheel. Practices lost their intensity, and our games felt like exhibitions, played because they were scheduled. Every once in a while we managed to win one, usually when another team failed to take us seriously.

Personally, I was playing decently. Building on Norrkoping, I continued to embrace personal success, and, in another encouraging sign, I no longer considered it dissonant to make money playing ball. Finally, I was at peace with having the highest salary on the team. Most importantly, when the team started losing, I knew better than to blame myself. Despite all the personal and pecuniary growth, I settled in, like everyone else, for the long grind of a losing season. But then, as always, came a call from Mike.

My phone rang, jolting me out of my glacial trance at the window. I stared at the string of numbers on the screen, the +1 USA indicating a NY area code.

"What's up Mike," I said.

"Ian, listen, there's a team in Hungary that wants you. The deal is really solid. It'd be your highest salary yet in Europe. Payments are reliable, and the game bonuses with this team are insane," Mike said. Given our place in the standings, he was certain that Gothenburg would release me from contract obligations and I could be in Hungary by mid-week.

"I don't know, man," I said, somewhat annoyed my tranquil evening had been interrupted by something so alluring.

Mike didn't ask for an answer right away. "Keep your

phone on."

A quick Google search of the Hungarian city of Paks doesn't reveal much. It's more of a small town, actually, with a population no bigger than 20,000, a good chunk of whom work in the nearby nuclear power facility. In Paks there's a diffuse scattering of agriculture ringing a tightly packed residential core containing several restaurants, a few bars, numerous tanning beds and hair salons, and, on the northern edge of the city, a basketball arena.

I was still clicking through Google results when Mike called me back. The team — Paks Atomeromu, Atomic Paks — had upped their offer, and I knew I'd accept it when I felt myself start to resist.

Less than twenty-four hours later, in the Gothenburg team offices, I signed out of the rest of my deal in Sweden. Almost in the same pen stroke, I signed a faxed copy of the new deal from Paks, and soon after that I was buckled into a 777 and accelerating out of Swedish airspace, the airplane's nose pointed over the Baltic Sea, destination Budapest's Ferenc Liszt International Airport. Beyond that lay another unknown chapter and verse of the emotionally wayward, geographical zig-zag that was becoming my professional basketball career.

My arrival in Paks coincided with a number of other personnel shake-ups the team had recently made, and our first game as a new unit took us to Budapest. We won, but our new parts weren't exactly gelling, and in the locker room afterwards the American contingent was making this clear. "Might as well pack it up now and go home," said Nick, our shooting guard from Cincinnati, as he tore off his uniform.

The Hungarians were talking harshly among themselves too, and the team president, the GM, and our Coach, Dzunic, stood by the door in their own tense huddle. I stayed quiet and looked at my feet, digesting my performance. I'd failed to start and scored 5 meager points, and had either forgotten my *Just don't give a fuck* mantra or it had lost its magic.

A few days later, in our second lap around the track, we played a team we needed to leapfrog in the playoff race. At halftime were down 15, and I had 3 points, all free throws, in just a few minutes off the bench.

In the huddle on the sideline just before the second half, Coach Dzunic informed the team there'd be a change in the starting five. He pointed at several players, paused a moment, then looked over at me and gave me a single nod. "And Ee-yan. You will start at four position."

Somewhat surprised, I nodded back, pulled off my warm-up, and bent over to re-lace my shoes.

Nick, tucking in his uniform, hovered over Coach Dzunic's shoulder. "Coach, wait, Ian?" he said, loud enough for everyone to hear. "You sure?"

When Coach ignored him, Nick addressed the whole team. "Yo, we're starting *Ian*," he said loudly, as if people hadn't heard the first time.

Whether it was Coach Dzunic's surprising booster shot in starting me or Nick's verbal slap across the ego, I don't know. A tandem dance of the two, perhaps. Whatever the cause, I was suddenly alive, and we rallied to start the second half and then pulled away down the stretch. Walking to the locker room after the game, a commanding victory in our pockets, Nick patted me on my shoulder and said, "We knew you had it in you, dawg."

I had it in me the next game, too, scoring 24 in my first contest in front of our home crowd, and from there all of a sudden we were harnessing this massively intense momentum, winning game after game, and nobody was talking about going home anymore.

When we did start to slip, the front office found ways to reignite us. In one important game, for example, we were down 8 points heading into halftime. On our heels as we filed into the locker room was the team president. Bumping Coach Dzunic out of the way, he bounced around the room shouting "Extra bonus! Extra bonus!" in both English and Hungarian. "If you win," he repeated, catching his breath, "big extra bonus." Coach Dzunic didn't have much to say after that.

In James Naismith's autobiography, he relates a conversation he had with a referee named "Fields," who told him that whenever he refereed a game he always made sure the window in his dressing room was unlocked, so that he'd have an escape route should he need it following a game.

In Naismith's time there was usually only one referee per game, who was often easily neutralized with a little cash or a well-worded threat. The game's caretakers recognized the need for a second referee, and eventually mandated one, but it was often the practice for leagues to supply one referee and then recruit a second referee from the city hosting the game, and the local referee, of course, was more or less a sixth man.

Before out-of-bounds rules were modified, gym managers often erected a wire netting, or cage, around the court to keep the ball in play (sparking the term "cagers"), which in basketball's early heathen era turned the game into a kind of UFC match. The referees, fearing for their safety, often only entered the cage during game stoppages, and would initiate play by tossing the ball in through a slit in the netting, like in foosball. A player throwing a ball inbounds would stand with his back against the cage, during which time front row fans could pinch, slap, extinguish cigarettes, pull leg hairs, and dump beer on opposing inbounders.

In a 1967 *Sports Illustrated* article about Doug Moe, a two-time All-American at the University of North Carolina, who, like Bill Bradley, was one of the first Americans to venture into overseas professional leagues, an Italian newspaper editor told the magazine, "It is all very simple. It is not only that the officials are incompetent. They are simply afraid of the fans, and rightly so. They have to rule for the home team or they'll spend the next two or three hours running for their lives."

Asked to comment on Italian fans, Moe said, "Sometimes I think they just come to the games for the exercise of fighting. Before a game there'll be three or four fights going on in the stands and everybody egging 'em on and nobody trying to stop 'em. Sometimes it's one long fight to get back into the dressing room. This Italian basketball — it's like an audience-participation sport."

Tragically, too often the audience becomes the story. In 1964, during an Olympic qualifying soccer match between Argentina and host Peru, at least three hundred people were killed and hundreds more injured when the referee invalidated what would've been a game-tying Peruvian goal in the game's closing minutes, inciting fans to storm the pitch. Peruvian police fired tear gas in an attempt to control the crowd, a move that instead prompted everyone to rush the exits to escape the gas. The exits, however, were initially locked, creating a bottleneck that was deadly enough to kill hundreds of people. In 1985, before a heated European Cup final between English powerhouse Liverpool and Italian giants Juventus, an escalade of taunting led the Liverpool fanbase to storm through a police line and rush their Juventus counterparts, eventually leading to the collapse of a wall, resulting in 39 dead and almost 400 injured.

In today's European professional leagues, from basketball to soccer to handball, hooliganism remains a part of the scene, but in a somewhat subdued form. The stadium collapses of the 20th century prompted infrastructure reform, and on a moral level appeals from higher-ups have somewhat simmered the most, ahem, passionate fans. Still, incidents of fan violence aren't uncommon. In Serbia, basketball games between Red Star Belgrade and Partizan Belgrade often dissolve into violent mosh pits of fan furor, with basketball, as Doug Moe put it, merely a convenient excuse to congregate and fight. And in Hungary in 2009, as my fellow Americans and I lead Paks to the top of the league, fans were reacting to our success in curious ways.

In late March, we played a road game in Dombovar, a city an hour or so from Budapest. While so-called security guards played possum, so-called fans ringed the court during warm-ups, cigarettes bobbing on their lips as they clogged lay-up lines and snarled insults. (Morbidly curious,

I pressed my Hungarian teammates to translate. Perhaps embarrassed, they mostly refused.) Alcohol fumes and tobacco smoke hung in the air like North Sea clouds on the coast of England, and when the game began I felt gladiatorial, like I was fighting to stay alive as much as I was playing to win. That's perhaps a shade melodramatic, but lining up during free throws I put my hands on my knees to lessen the likelihood of an object hitting my head, and during extended stoppages in play (like when Nick, perhaps our best player, somehow received two flagrant fouls in the first quarter and was subsequently ejected), I tried to stand as close to the other team's big men as I could, hoping fans would be less willing to risk hitting one of their own guys with a battery or coin.

In Game 2 of the semi-finals in the 2009 Hungarian Playoffs, in which we squared off against Falco, my team, Paks, jumped out to a big early lead. We held that lead until the fourth quarter, when Falco streaked back. Falco's fans, silenced for three and a half quarters, suddenly lit up, the arena growing so loud with every home team bucket that it eventually felt quiet, like I'd been knocked out.

Falco had just about pulled even with a minute left, but on our next possession I was fouled driving to the basket. Their coach was assessed a technical foul arguing the call, which gave us four free throws. I knocked one of two down, and Nick, shooting the technicals, hit both, putting us up three.

The technical meant we'd keep possession, and after a timeout one of our players inbounded to Nick behind half court. Nick dribbled around up top for several seconds, drove left and, cut off by a help defender, kicked it to me on the wing, where I pulled up for a long three. *Swish!*

My three put our team up 6 points with less than thirty seconds to play. The crowd, so recently a jet engine, went silent as quick as a mute button. Falco had fought so hard to get close, but now, instead of heading back to Paks for Game 3 with the series tied 1-1, we were set to go up 2-0, and there was no way my teammates and I would choke on a two-game lead. In essence, then, that little sequence decided the series.

Not giving up, Falco quickly inbounded to their point guard, who rushed down the left side of the court, hoping to get a quick shot and spark a miracle. Our point guard, Mike, pressured him, and just past half-court their feet became entangled. Both players fell to the floor. Both sprang up, nose to nose, and that was it. Tick, boom!

For the record, Falco started it. Instantaneously, half of their bench, totally in unison, rifled from their seats, heading straight for Mike. At the same time, a slew of their fans, also eerily in unison, as if all under the same spell, stormed over the advertisements that bordered the sideline and rushed across the court, targeting anyone wearing Paks red. Their battalion, according to newspaper estimates the next day, numbered fifty or sixty. All men.

A third group rushed the court a half-second later: security. It took a minute, but they got everyone separated, and important people started doing what important people do in situations like this — stand around and talk. After several minutes of discussion, the game was called, the twenty-odd remaining seconds scratched, the victory ours. Not playing out the game wasn't totally a precaution, as even if we'd wanted to play, we'd have had no refs. One had gotten punched by a fan, after which all three refused to retake the court.

A classic psych experiment from the late 1890s went like this: A gunman enters a crowded theater, fires his weapon, and then quickly runs out. The lights come on immediately after the gunman exits, and several policemen arrive to gather eyewitness accounts. The theater attendees don't know it, but the whole thing is staged. The gunman is an accomplice (though the gunshots were real), and the "police" are actually the study's authors.

The theatergoers, the psychologists found, gave widely varying reports about the event. Some said two shots were fired, others one or three, while a few couldn't remember a shot at all. Some said there were two gunmen, not one, and many others reported that the gunman had been chasing someone. Some said the gunman was tall with brown hair, while others said he was overweight with a black hat. The conclusion, the psychologists claimed, is that memory is not literal and objective, as we tend to think, but reconstructive and subjective. It is, at root, a form of imagination.

In the rear of the bus on the way back from Falco, Mike, Nick and Charles and I (our American contingent) dissected the brawl, piecing together what we thought had happened. The animated voices from the Hungarians up front suggested they were doing the same. Like the witnesses in the theater, our memories seemed wholly subjective — all we could agree on was that *something* had happened — but, unlike the theater-goers, we would find out what, as the next day before practice, manhoods on the line, we gathered for our regular post-game video session.

Nobody cared about the actual game. My teammates and I nodded along impatiently, and nervously, as Dzunic did his thing. Then came the game's final minute, the spillage of drunken men onto the court, the rush of security and the overlay of confusion. Everyone tensed up and leaned forward.

Allow me to share how immensely fascinating it is to watch yourself in a brawl. You fancy yourself a certain kind of guy, someone who'd stand up for himself and others, a sentiment the video, stoically neutral, will either confirm or deny. The night before, as I'd lay in bed, I'd replayed how I thought I'd reacted with how I wanted to think I'd reacted, hoping they overlapped.

The video rolled on. Never before or since had I been in so tense a film room, not even at Davidson. You could see Mike and Falco's point guard step towards each other, nose to nose. You could see Falco's bench clear. You watched one of their players leap through the air, fist extended, and drill Mike in the temple (his nickname became "Superman"). You saw the onrush of fans from the top of the picture, a stampede of frustration and unclear intentions. You saw several wild punches thrown, a few connecting, then the arrival of security and wiser heads. You saw most of the Hungarians on our bench do nothing but stare, a condition which did not sit well with Mike. Before the tape could finish, Mike erupted at them, letting loose a barrage of "pussies," "soft-ass bitches," and many more nuggets that won't make the book.

And what about me? As the brawl unfolded, I wrapped my arms around Falco's center, who was charging after Mike, and held him back. I held him for maybe three seconds before being forced to let go, as over my shoulder I'd noticed a crew of men rushing towards me. To this day I can quite vividly recall the sensation, how eerily calm I became, the withdrawn internal sigh, as I prepared to engage them. I even remember the thought that crossed my mind: *Well, if I gotta fight, I gotta fight.* They closed the distance and my fists clenched, but their rush slowed and then stopped, dispersing and dispensing around me, like a river around an island, in search of other targets, namely Nick, Charles, and Mike, all of whom are African-American.

Game 3 was back in Paks. In the aftermath of the melee the referees had threatened to strike, and in response the league issued a written warning to the coaches and players on both teams — so much as blink in a way that offends the refs and face ejection, suspension, and quite possibly, electrocution.

The warning worked. The game passed pleasantly in church-like conditions. Fans clapped as if dressed to their Sunday nines at a polo match in Uptownshire near a sunny lake dotted with golden swans. Although not many churches, I suppose, feature police squadrons in full riot gear standing shoulder-to-shoulder up and down the aisles. It felt almost like a semi-formal, not a semi-final. I hit five three pointers as we won the game and clinched the series, punching our ticket to the championship round of the Nemzeti Bajnokság, the Hungarian Finals.

For several minutes before Game 1 of the Hungarian Finals, against our opponent Pecs, I couldn't catch my breath. This might've been nerves, or it might've been an actual dearth of oxygen, as Pecs had either overestimated the seating capacity of its arena or was paying the fire department to look the other way. I felt claustrophobic even on the court, the arena like a thundercloud, everything electrically charged.

For nearly every team that plays in a competitive league most anywhere in the world, the season ends with a loss. Every season I'd played in since high school had ended in failure: failure to win the Southern Conference tournament, failure to win the NIT, failure in the NCAAs, failure in the Czech Republic, failure in the playoffs with Norrkoping. I was used to a grim and glum locker room come a season's final buzzer, and given that only one team can win a title at a time, most athletes, I imagine, are used to the same.

After warm-ups we retreated to the locker room for our final preparations.

"Let's get these motherfuckers," Nick said.

"Let's get that money," Charles chimed in.

"Let's take what's ours," I added.

Coach Dzunic stepped up to address the team, but he didn't have to say much. We could feel the hostility of the arena even down where we were, and we knew, or at least could sense, all that was at stake. We'd been thinking about this moment since February, when we'd won our first game together as a new unit and realized how good we could be.

Trophies, reputations, championship bonuses, future contracts, the feeling of general life satisfaction, the privilege of saying, "Yes, I won a championship," at cocktail parties and backyard barbecues long after we'd retired — all of this was in play. We were either ready or we weren't.

The pregame electricity hadn't subsided when we retook the court. Our center and their center lined up in the middle of the circle, and the referee tossed up the jump ball. I won the tip, passed it to our point guard, Mike, and Game 1 was underway.

Most of the game was played in a state of heightened, palatable tension. We were nervous, the other team was nervous, the fans were drunk and crazy. But we were ready. At twenty-five, I was the youngest member of our starting five. All of us had taken a few laps around the track, so to speak, and our veteran professionalism and composure were unmatched. We were down double-digits at the start of the second half, but we used a big run at the start of the third to take the lead, and held on down the stretch. I hit the dagger with ten seconds left from almost the same spot where I hit the riot-sparking game winner in the semifinals against Falco ten days earlier. This time, however, the fans stayed in their seats, and we went home up 1-0.

Game 2 was at our place in Paks, and we hadn't lost at home since the team was restructured five months earlier. This game was closer than the first, however, and we didn't secure the win until we grabbed the rebound off their miss in the final seconds.

Game 3 was an easy win, at least compared to the first two. We were too physically disciplined and mentally tough to allow a team to come back from two games down in a best of five, and Pecs seemed to have given up. All we needed to do was execute, and we did. So as the final minutes of Game 3 of the Finals ticked down, a game we'd convincingly won to sweep the series, the lightness I felt as I ran out those final seconds was as much about not finishing the season with a loss as it was about securing the championship with a win. It was like discovering an extra room in your favorite home, full of strange family heirlooms you never knew were there.

Any meaningful success, however, is bittersweet. Bitter because what truly is sweet are the steps to the championship, not the glory in its wake. A trophy is just a trophy, a stylish molding of gold or platinum that means nothing until one confers upon it a certain value, and that value can only be measured by the toil and tears it took to earn it.

On the ride home from Pecs to Paks, bottles were emptied and new ones opened, the bus leaning precariously to one side as we circled and re-circled the roundabouts. Halfway home we stopped at a restaurant to buy more alcohol. The chartered buses carrying our fans stopped, too, and the trophy was filled with beer. Everyone sipped heartily from it, though I passed on the opportunity. So did Charles.

"Nasty," he said.

"Yeah, man, gross," I echoed, and we both giggled like little boys.

Foreign players in European leagues, particularly Americans, are typically the first to be blamed when a team fails. This is perhaps appropriate, as Americans are usually hired to be the team's best players. When a team succeeds, however, the Americans don't always receive credit to a corresponding degree, but this is likewise appropriate, as in most cases American players make more money than their European counterparts. They are also the most transient members of the team, the most eager to bolt for a better deal. But, inevitably, American players gravitate to each other, hoping for the best, and it is often with one's fellow expats that the strongest bonds can be formed.

After practices in Paks, the other Americans and I would strap ice bags to our knees, sip Gatorade and discuss the important issues of the day. After the "big bonus" game, for instance, we discussed with some seriousness whether we should try to deliberately fall behind at halftime in future games, in hopes of luring the president back into the locker room with promises of more cash. When we weren't being conspiratorial, we debated which CNN International anchors we most wanted to date (I was fond of Anjali Rao), whether the waiter at our meal-a-day restaurant ever flicked cigarette ashes into our food, and at what age and in what fashion each of our Hungarian teammates had lost his virginity.

One topic we never discussed was the way our relationship with each other affected our play. Did our chumminess bring out the best in each other? Correlation is obviously not causation, but my best seasons as a pro were the seasons when I got along best with my American teammates, when I played less for the coach or the fans and most for the brothers with whom I shared a nationality. And with no team throughout my career did I play better than I did in Paks. Maybe feeling like I deserved success wasn't such a big mystery after all. Maybe it was simply finding teammates whom I wouldn't dare let down.

On the summer afternoon of June 4th, 1923, five horses set off in a steeplechase race at New York's Belmont Park. The favorite, Gimme, was upstaged by Sweet Kiss, a 20-to-1 long shot ridden by a jockey named Frank Hayes. As they rounded the final turn, Sweet Kiss nearly ran into Gimme before straightening out, pulling ahead and winning by a length and a half. According to a *New York Times* recap the following day, as the horses slowed to a trot past the finish line, Hayes fell off his horse and tumbled to the dirt below, where he lay motionless.

Hayes wasn't a jockey as much as he was a trainer. He'd never won a race before, and to prepare for the Belmont he'd initiated a rapid weight loss plan that saw him lose twelve pounds in a matter of days. A doctor's postmortem suggested the weight loss, coupled with the day's excitement, contributed to the heart failure that struck him at some point during the race. He never got up from the track that day, and a few days later was buried in full racing regalia at a nearby cemetery. His horse was apparently renamed "Sweet Kiss of Death," and Hayes remains the only jockey to go out a winner after losing his life.

Death, of course, can come at any time, from a bullet to the aorta or from an overdose of heroin, or simply from a misfired electric impulse in the cerebellum while sleeping peacefully. Or from having a 400 pound log fall on you in preseason football camp (Josh Mileto, 16, Farmingville, NY, 2017), from head trauma after getting hit in the head by a spitball (Ray Chapman, Cleveland Indians, 1920), or from a brain hemorrhage after having your head slammed into the ice (Bill Masterton, Minnesota North Stars, 1968).

Of the four major sports leagues in the United States — NBA, MLB, NFL, NHL — the NBA is the only one not to have had one of its players die from a cause directly relating to the game itself. For instance, no NBA player has ever hit his head on the hardwood and died as a result. The NBA, however, has seen a number of players collapse on the court and expire from a more hidden threat, heart failure, with Reggie Lewis (1993) and Jason Collier (2005) serving as the most notable tragic examples. Another would-be NBA player, Hank Gathers of Loyola Marymount University, just the second player in Division 1 history to lead the nation in scoring and rebounding, died of a heart condition after collapsing during a game in 1990. Many less notable players, from Australia to Austria to Atlanta, have met the same fate.

I'd had occasional heart murmurs while playing for Paks. Or maybe they were palpitations; I still don't know the difference, if there is one. Whatever they were, they felt like a large butterfly flapping in the cavity of my ribcage, and I usually experienced them laying down for a nap or going to sleep at night. Frightened death was imminent, I did what any sensible young man would do in the face of such fears: ignored them. Within a few minutes, after rolling over or sitting up for a while, they usually went away.

One night in late June 2009, a few days after returning home to Virginia from Paks, I opened the refrigerator, pulled out a big slice of pesto pizza and watched it rotate in the microwave until the cheese bubbled. A few minutes later, I wiped tomato sauce from my mouth and loaded the dishwasher, trod upstairs, brushed my teeth and lay down with a book. A half-hour after that, I flipped off the light and rolled on my side, ready for sleep. As I lay in bed, the heart murmurs returned with an impact impossible to ignore. Never before had they been so violent. I waited a few minutes to be sure, then crept down to my parent's bedroom, where, feeling like a five year old with a nightmare, I informed them that a hospital visit might be in good order.

My dad dutifully drove me to the emergency room, where I was admitted right away.

"Wow, you're tall," the nurse said as she handed me an aspirin and a small cup of water.

The ER staff drew blood and queried me from a stack of checklists. Did I smoke? Drink alcohol? What was my profession?

"I'm a basketball player," I ventured tremulously, as if this sealed my fate.

I was ushered into a big room with a big noisy machine that ran dye through my veins, and a few hours after that, the doctor had a diagnosis. I sat on the exam table, ready to go numb. My dad looked on, arms crossed. The doctor started talking. My heart was fine. I was not dying (any faster than usual), nor was my heart enlarged or beating arrhythmically. I'd been suffering, rather, from heartburn. "Stay away from spicy things," the doctor instructed. "Chew slowly, don't eat too much, and not before bed. Try to wait at least three hours after your last meal before lying down," he said sternly.

Not long after my visit to the ER, I happened to read *Skinny Bitch*, the best-selling go-vegan manifesto by Rory Freedman and Kim Barnouin. In saucy language, the book describes animal rights abuses in factory farms and raises the relevant environmental concerns associated with diet, but the most elaborated upon go-vegan sections cry out directly to your personal health. There are, apparently, a lot of reasons why factory-farmed animal products are bad for you, especially for people with stomachs sensitive to acid reflux. I read the book in an afternoon and vowed to give up meat and dairy on the spot.

In late July 2009, I signed with a team in Kecskemet, a city forty-five minutes southeast of Budapest, and that August I arrived in Europe for my fourth professional season largely free of the usual hiccups I'd come to expect with new European gigs. I was also free of the twenty or so pounds I'd lost since my trip to the hospital, the result of not eating before bed anymore and impulsively going vegan for the summer.

That first afternoon in Kecskemet, in the mirror of my new teammates, standing shoulder to shoulder with the men I used to look like, my weight loss centered in an uneasy spotlight. It felt like the first wisps of what would be my ultimate test as an athlete, one in which I'd have to choose between present-day success on the court and my long-term health off it.

Despite existential concerns about my weight, for the first half of the season I was relatively happy. I lived in a cozy, very agreeable apartment downtown. Save for the arena, which was just outside the city, I could comfortably walk anywhere: to the little grocery store with impossible labels, to the city plazas with their outdoor cafes and prime people-watching vantages, to a mall with a bookstore (English section) and a movie theater (English subtitles), to a few decent restaurants and to a few small bars and clubs, where, in one of my lesser-known but more affecting European accomplishments, I introduced Kecskemet to the SoCo and lime (You're welcome, Hungary!).

One night while out with the team, our starting 3-man walked up to the bar and asked for thirty-six rum and cokes. The bartender looked dubious, but my teammate slapped several hundred Euros on the bar and repeated his order.

"Why thirty-six?" I asked him as the bartender reached under the counter for a new bottle.

My teammate shrugged. "It's a good number," he said. When all thirty-six drinks were lined up on the bar, he beamed and downed one, made that pleased wincing look that drinkers give after swallowing, and set his empty glass off to the side. "Thirty-five." He handed me two, and I ventured off to find a lady to share the surplus with.

During the first few years of the 20th century, basketball at the University of Illinois was played only by women, usually in the loft of the school's Natural History Building. Male students liked to sneak up to the loft to watch the girls play, and often by the end of the night there was a lot more going on than just basketball. Word of this made its way to the school president, who subsequently banned basketball on school grounds altogether.

In its nascent years basketball was played as much by women as by men, encouraged, if somewhat erroneously, by founding father James Naismith, who wrote, "It has been found valuable for girls and women, as there are few games which they can play that are not a strain on the nervous system rather than on bodily functions. It is peculiarly adapted for giving health without involving severe mental strain."

In the 1890s Clara Baer, a physical education instructor at Sophie Newcomb College in New Orleans, was intrigued by reports of the new sport sweeping across New England, and she wrote to Naismith asking for advice and clarification on how to play. Naismith replied with a full explanation, replete with diagrams describing the different "zones" of the court where players should stand for the jump ball. Baer, however, misinterpreted the diagram, and when she published the first set of basketball rules for women in 1896 (which she renamed basquette) they included the directive that women players were to stay in certain zones the entire time they were on the court. A guard, for instance, would always stay in the back third of the court, always defending the basket and never crossing into the other two thirds, a restriction on player movement that would stay in place in some areas as late as the 1960s. Baer's rules are also noteworthy for their restriction of two-handed passes (for fear they would compress the chest) and for describing the jump shot, which wouldn't popularize in the men's game for another thirty years.

Baer's interpretations of the game echoed guidelines for women that were already in place up north, informally instituted in 1892 by Senda Berenson, a Lithuanian-born PE teacher at Massachusetts' Smith College who was friendly with Naismith in Springfield. Berenson's rules, like Baer's, reflected the Victorian feminine ideals of the time, prohibiting female players from ripping the ball from one another and likewise forcing them to stay put in specific zones, even going as far as to mandate players wear their hair in braids or ribbons to maintain a dignified appearance.

When Berenson organized the first official women's basketball game at Smith in 1893, the players wore bloomers and no male spectators were permitted to watch. The fans that did attend — exclusively the female classmates of the participants — were instructed to show their enthusiasm only through singing; any shouting would stop the match.

While Berenson was an unapologetic proponent of

physical education for women (among other ventures, she would later introduce basketball to inmates at the nearby Northampton Lunatic Asylum), she felt that the focus of athletics should "encourage the instinct of play, not competition," and used her influence as chairwoman of the United States Basket-Ball Committee, a post she held from 1905 to 1917, to limit women's college basketball to *intra*-activities.

While the women's game as its own entity would simmer in its restrictive rules for decades to come, finally opening up in the 60s and 70s under the direction of new pioneers like Tennessee coach Pat Summitt, women nonetheless continued to influence the men's game in more subtle ways.

Phog Allen, widely considered to be the father of basketball coaching, wrote in the first half of the 20th century a number of hugely influential books, including *My Basket Ball Bible,* which helped shift the game from a player-run sport to a coach-led institution. Except Phog didn't actually write the books; they were ghostwritten by his wife, Bessie. The extent to which Phog dictated to her the contents is unknown, but we can reasonably presume that she wasn't just a mentally inert typist.

There is always a significant other, or lack of one, and for better or worse, off-court relationships have always had and will always have a "Tim Duncian" impact on on-court performance.

In Kecskemet I became involved with two significant others. The first was Lena, the woman to whom I delivered the extra rum and coke in broken Hungarian. She worked as a schoolteacher but was a former dancer, and could still relate to the athlete's grind. She didn't speak English very well and I didn't speak much Hungarian, but we both spoke a little German, and auf Deutsch we were able to forge a small relationship, a relationship that we enjoyed for a number of months because we knew going in that it would never last. Our relationship was basic arithmetic, both of us committing low integers and demanding nothing more than simple addition, me plus her for one or two nights a week.

Together we'd cook dinner and take turns reading aloud in English or German, giving each other lists of vocab words to study as we went along. When we both had days off we'd drive out to her parents' place a little ways into the country, where we'd go for bike rides or walk or just lay out in the grass. There was always food hidden under a checkered blanket draped over the big table in her mother's kitchen.

With Lena, I was funny, relaxed, and spontaneous, at ease with myself and at peace with the world. I didn't feel alone, and this healthy companionship off the court positively affected my play on it. But then Lena and I started to like each other, and as soon as real life got involved, things became weird and we quickly broke up.

In early January, my head coach in Kecskemet, Coach Levente, approached me before practice. "Eyan, congratulation," he said, "you make All-Star team."

I stood there for a second, digesting this, then nodded and looked around, hoping nobody else could hear. I told Coach Levente that was good news and then quickly scooted back into warm-ups. By the end of practice I was convinced there'd been a mistake, just like there'd been a mistake in my making the All-Star team in Norrkoping. I cycled through players on other teams, thinking a large number of them must've been injured, but everyone seemed to be relatively healthy. Even though I recognized its irrationality, I told myself that the league's front office must've conspired to put me on the team, for vague but probably pity-related reasons.

After practice it was my turn to approach Coach. "Thank you," I said sheepishly, grinning as if I was now in on the joke.

"Thank you what?" he said in his thick Eastern European accent.

"The All-Star team. Whatever you did, thank you for getting me on there."

He looked bewildered. "What you mean?"

I studied his expression. I knew that to further explain myself would be to reveal more of me than I wanted to reveal, and so I said never mind and headed for the locker room, where I prayed my teammates hadn't found out.

A few days after the All-Star game, I drove to a parking lot not far from the arena. There was only one other car there, half-hidden in the lot's urban shadows, occupied by one of the team's assistant coaches. I stepped out of my car and plunked down in his passenger seat. He wordlessly handed me a thick envelope full of American dollars, my monthly payment, and told me to count it. When I arrived at the correct number, I thanked him, got back in my car and drove away. This was how we were paid, covertly and in cash.

So I was getting paid and playing well, but something was

still missing, if not in my condition as a whole, then in how I wholly saw my condition. At the beginning of my career all I'd wanted was consistency with my personal game and stability in my professional situation. Now that I had those things, it seemed they weren't enough, that they were never what I'd really sought in the first place.

In the fall of my senior year at Davidson I took Clinical Psychopharmacology, a high-level psychology class in which we studied different mental illnesses and discussed their treatments. About halfway through the syllabus we arrived at obsessive-compulsive disorder, and as my professor described OCD I had the incredibly strange sensation that he was, in fact, describing me. For the entire week I daydreamed about raising my hand and offering to serve as a real-life example, but I could never fully understand why I was so tempted. I was aware that it's natural for people to falsely see themselves in the medical descriptions they read about, and so relegated to a lower shelf the idea that I might be suffering from something diagnosable.

Margery Kempe, living at the end of the 14th century and considered by many to have written the first autobiography in English, spent good portions of her book describing what appear to be obsessive thoughts of a religious and sexual nature (Kempe was illiterate and dictated her story to a scribe):

"...so had she now horrible sights and abominable, for aught she could do, of beholding men's members, and such other abominations. She saw, as she thought verily, diverse men of religion, priests and many others, both heathen and Christian, coming before her sight, so that she might not eschew them or put them out of her sight, showing their bare members unto her..."

John Bunyan, who in 1678 wrote *Pilgrim's Progress*, considered to be one of the most important Christian texts ever, detailed in his own autobiography the overwhelming extent of his obsessive fears, writing "These things may seem ridiculous to others, even as ridiculous as they were in themselves, but to me tormenting cogitations."

As the season in Kecskemet progressed, I grew increasingly haunted by the "tormenting cogitations" of obsessive-compulsive disorder, which assaulted me with a severity I'd never known. Ninety percent of the time I ran up and down the court I staggered my stride to avoid stepping on the half-court line. When I could, I avoided stepping on any line, even though a basketball court is well-mapped by them. I turned twenty-six in Kecskemet, a year that I feared would be my last, as age twenty-seven had claimed the lives of so many prominent people — Janis Joplin, Jimi Hendrix, Jim Morrison, Kurt Cobain, Reggie Lewis — and I feared I was next. To compensate, I tried to hold my post-practice stretches for at least twenty-eight seconds, as if the twenty-eight seconds would correspond to living to at least twenty-eight years of age. If I forgot or miscounted, I would count to twenty-eight as fast as I could, in fear that my heart would stop if I didn't do it quickly enough. The list of symptoms goes on and on, but I'm trying to keep this book to one volume.

By April my OCD had ramped up so viciously that I was concerned I wouldn't live to the end of the season. I recognized some of the same self-canceling impulses I'd experienced at Davidson, the same impulses I'd felt off and on my entire life, and although I can't remember formulating a specific plan, most of my days became what I would eventually call "lightswitch days." These were days during which, even if I wouldn't make the full effort to kill myself, I still would, if presented with a magical switch that would end my life, willingly reach out and flip off the light.

Throughout my career, I discovered that one of the silver linings of getting physically injured was that I could admit I was in pain. On occasion, nursing a twisted ankle or bad bruise, I sometimes felt myself not wanting to heal, simply because I wanted to keep saying, "I'm hurt." But unlike Kempe and Bunyan, who could at least describe their symptoms, I couldn't admit the pain of the injuries that nobody could see. And if I couldn't admit my injuries, then the unresolved emotions would symptomize in obsessions and compulsions, all the way up until the moment when I would make those symptoms go away, one way or another.

It had never been easy for me to go bed. Among other things, I viscerally feared the moment when I would lose consciousness. In Kecskemet I would lay with my eyes closed, curled up under the covers, exhausted beyond comprehension, yet unable to drift off into sleep because I feared that once I did I would never wake up. If I didn't go to sleep, I wouldn't die, went my logic.

My pre-bedtime routine intensified, adding new layers to an already draining affair. I started with music, requiring myself to listen to a certain number of songs a certain number of times, until things felt "right." Then I'd have to walk "correctly" across the apartment to the bathroom, where I'd have to brush my teeth "correctly," and then I'd have to check the locks on my front door and look through the peephole a certain number of times, and then it was a certain number of footsteps to bed, where I'd lay, heart pounding, until I got back up and checked the door again. Any sort of negative thought — thoughts about dying or not playing well, for instance — disqualified everything and I'd have to restart all the way back with the music.

 The catalyst for the shift from a relatively stable existence to a dangerously suicidal one was the second woman I dated in Kecskemet. That winter, I'd quickly and unexpectedly entered into a relationship with Emma, a Canadian volleyball player I'd met on a trip to Budapest. Emma and I were perhaps a good match on paper — both tall professional athletes — but, unlike my healthier (and briefer) relationships with European women, like Lena, which had mostly unfolded on the surface, this one was largely commanded by the unconscious and trauma-haunted depths of our psyches. Like me, Emma's brain was kind of tangled, and neither of us knew how to ask for help, or even to acknowledge that we needed it. Emma didn't live in Hungary, she'd just been visiting, and the everyday challenges of a long-distance relationship, the insecurities and jealousies, were compounded by the acerbity of my obsessive-compulsive symptoms.

One afternoon I dropped to my knees by the kitchen sink and in what I can only see as a form of prayer, asked for help. I sunk to the ground and lay like a pile of limp laundry, wishing I could cry. I was on fire, and I was done straddling the edge; I was either going to get better or turn off the light once and for all. I struggled to sit up, and then to stand. I grabbed my bag and keys. Practice started in an hour. Assuming I didn't jump out of a window or run my car into oncoming traffic on the way, I was pretty sure I'd be there.

Part II - The Echo

Chapter 7 — Recovery Part One

For many athletes, if not most, the decision to retire isn't an easy one, even if it's the most obvious and logical and irreversible path forward. This decision is agonized over, often for years, compounded by the fact that most athletes reach their personal peak without ever harvesting the sense of total accomplishment that only the rarest of athletes are lucky enough to ever feel. Every athlete, in a way, quits early.

Put another way, every player dreams of being an alpha at the highest level, but very few are ever good enough to get there. Every player will, one day, inevitably fall back to Earth and no longer be an athlete. Retired athletes become, by and large, books abandoned before the climax, movie reels ripped from the projector before the third act, or canvases removed from the easel before the image can fully take shape. That they were lucky enough to sit on the easel or have been loaded into the projector in the first place is of little consolation at the end, because from the time athletes first pick up a ball they're instructed never to be satisfied with who they are at any given moment. Instead, they're instructed to be in constant pursuit of an almost unattainable future self.

So when, at the end, they're all of a sudden dumped outside the theater, surrounded by a pile of half-finished scripts in the shadow of a life they're no longer a part of, constipated with unresolved feelings for their former sport, the inevitable reflective thought is one of failure.

On May 13th, 2011, at the end of my fifth season in Europe, I suited up for what would be my last game as a professional basketball player. At the time, I wasn't all that concerned with how I'd feel at the end of the game, whether I'd consider my career a success or not. After the events of the previous couple years, I was simply glad I'd made it there alive.

It was easier to ask for help in Kecskemet than it had been at Davidson years before, if only because I was that much more desperate. There were entire days when suicide felt like an inevitability, days where I'd wake up and ask myself what I was still doing alive. When I dropped to my knees in surrender that afternoon before practice, I managed to lift myself up, and before I left for the gym I took advantage of a brief moment of resolve to log onto Skype and call my sister. By this point she'd been sober for almost four years, and we'd steadily repaired our relationship. I wasn't quite ready to tell her I was thinking of smashing my head in with a cast iron skillet (my suicidal ideations were often gruesome, designed to require my complete commitment), but I did mention that my thoughts had felt a little funny recently and did she know any therapists who might talk to me long-distance? My sister dutifully gave me a number, and I called that therapist right there and then, not trusting myself to maintain my resolve.

"So what's been going on," the therapist said during our first phone session several days later. I proceeded to speak for forty-five uninterrupted minutes.

"Sounds like you've been holding in a lot," the therapist said at the end of our session.

In our subsequent phone sessions I worked to unload what I'd for decades worked so hard to keep buried. My initial therapy was focused more on acknowledging my issues than curing them, but I was holding the stat sheet in my hands, if you will, and allowing myself to look at it. And the more I looked, it seemed, the less I wanted to play basketball.

After my season in Kecskemet ended, I flew to Winnipeg to spend the summer with Emma, the Canadian volleyball player I'd met at the bar in Budapest. That July I resigned in Hungary, and in early September I flew back to Europe with Emma. The life of a professional basketball player is often full of free time, especially so when you live in a small town and don't drink or go out anymore, as was the case with Emma and me in Hungary. We watched movies and adopted a foster dog, but mostly I read. Suddenly aware of how desperate I was to *know,* I began to devour books. My consumption of the written word would mark the beginning of my re-education, an ultra-autodidactic period of my life that would shape the rest of it to come. Some of my affinity for words at the time was born out of mere curiosity, and some of it was simply a way to fill the empty hours, but it also felt at times as if I was unwittingly preparing myself to step out of a bubble. When I stopped playing, I would have to figure out how to live all over again, and with every book I read it became more clear that I'd never really acquired a proper education. Just like with therapy, the more I read, the less it felt like I wanted to play basketball.

Emma and I spent Christmas in Paris, France where, sitting in a little cafe on the Rue de Rivoli in the 2nd arrondissement, just before attending a riveting performance of Ave Maria at the Eglise Saint-Gervais, I told her I would retire from professional basketball at the end of the season. I'd considered quitting as early as Gijon, and had assessed my future constantly throughout my career, but my deliberations had always been private. I'd never declared my intention to retire aloud before — had never had the courage — but I was in the early stages of my re-education and was armed with a budding sense of self. I was just about ready to start dictating my life on my own terms, and basketball, for now, wouldn't (*couldn't*) be a part of it.

My last season was largely successful, and my team spent portions of it atop the league before sliding down to fourth place. Throughout, I played with both the freedom and the timidity of someone who knows the end is near. The last game of our season, the last of my career, was played on a dark day in May. A lone gray cloud seemed to follow the team bus from the hotel to the gym, parking itself ominously above the arena.

On the court, my mind detached from my body, and I played the first half with my consciousness hovering somewhere over my left shoulder. When my mind did communicate with my body, it was my mind telling my body not to get hurt.

In the locker room at halftime I found myself calculating, as a percentage, how much of my career I had left. I tallied the number of games I'd played each season, starting with my senior year of high school and up through four years at Davidson and five abroad. The two quarters left in Kormend, or so went my estimate, signified the remaining point two percent of my basketball career — more than I expected. That the percentage would soon be zero was surreal to me, impossible to understand in percentages or otherwise.

In the second half, the thought of unnecessarily blowing a knee so close to the end deterred any lingering urge I possessed to compete. A three-point attempt from the far right wing was my last official statistic. As soon as that shot bricked, Coach Istvan pointed to a player on the bench, and at the next dead ball (how appropriate a phrase in this instance), I slapped that player's hand, walked to the end of the bench, put on my warm-up top and sat down. And that was it. There would be no game-winner for me, no retirement ceremony, or a standing ovation from an adoring crowd. Not all of us can go out like Jordan over Russell, one's follow-through held aloft for perpetuity. Or like Jeter, smacking a walk-off and cementing a legacy at the end of a year of over-the-top farewell tours in every ballpark in America. Some of us simply go out, as silently as a candle. You fade and fade, imperceptibly, and you don't notice you're gone until you look to see you're no longer there. And you really are gone, when you retire, as an athlete is all you've ever really known yourself to be. Immediately after my final professional game, expecting to feel relieved, I was instead greeted by the numb sense that I had, despite my lifelong investment in the game, somehow failed.

Sports do not usually involve literal life-and-death situations, but sports are nonetheless a proxy for death-related sentiments. When athletes compete, both teams may walk off the court at the end of the game in one piece. But if everyone involved identifies with their sport, and if everyone needs to win to establish or reinforce that identity, then competition is, at root, a battle to kill off your competitor's identity before they take yours. But what happens to your identity when there are no more games to play? This is the crux of retirement: *What can I do when I no longer know how to feel alive?*

The most shocking thing about my retirement was that I didn't immediately feel happy the second it commenced. I'd expected to feel happy because I'd wrongly assumed that basketball was the reason for my unhappiness. Basketball, I didn't yet know, had been my crutch, a life vest that protected me through life's roughest waters. By retiring, I was declaring that I was ready to continue the path of self-discovery that I'd aborted again and again over the years.

All major U.S. professional sports leagues offer lucrative pension plans to their players, but obviously very few athletes ever play in those leagues. Pension plans in European and U.S. semi-professional leagues are virtually non-existent, and college and high school athletes often walk away deeply in debt. (College athletes are supposedly armed with an education, which is claimed to be an insurance policy, but that's largely a farce.) Regardless, even if every athlete was privy to some massive retirement fund, arming retired athletes with cash does little to ensure a healthy transition away from their sport. Starting a new career doesn't ensure a healthy transition, either, as a new job is often simply a cover-up, a new way of making money. For an athlete to truly retire, the first step is for that former athlete to accept that he or she is truly dead. (One of the easiest ways to get a read on a former athlete is to ask them about their playing days and then look to see if their eyes go waxy, if their body posture shifts, and if they change the way they talk. What you see in that moment is the ghost. That player has not really died.)

Not wanting to die, the first thing many athletes do in

retirement is choose to unretire. The most famous retirement/comeback story belongs of course to Michael Jordan, who retired from basketball in 1993 to play Major League Baseball, then returned to the NBA a year later, then re-retired from the NBA in 1998 only to return with the Washington Wizards in 2001, before (officially) retiring for the last time in 2003. Jordan, in essence, spent many years chasing a ghost. Trickle down from Jordan and the retirement landscape is littered with comebacks, both successful and unsuccessful, by athletes who tell their spouses "it's over" before blurting out "I'm in" the second a GM calls and asks if they have anything left. For hundreds of thousands more, nobody calls, but these athletes nevertheless train and wait and train and wait, tragically churning on a treadmill of infutility, incapable of turning their backs on hope, which is to say they're incapable of giving up on who they think they are.

A few days after I announced my retirement, Mike called and told me a team in France was looking for a post player, and if this call had come a couple weeks later, when I wasn't mentally burnt out after a long season in Hungary, I probably would've said yes, as despite all my therapy and newfound education, I was as addicted as any other ingrained athlete to the idea of being me.

If the retired athlete's first instinct is to unretire, his second instinct, the next-best way of keeping himself alive, is to play historian. Very few athletes are ever truly satisfied with their careers while they're playing, as satisfaction is largely seen, and rightly so, as detrimental to drive and focus. Operating under a parent-approved, society-sanctioned, media-perpetrated guise of "motivation," players and coaches know that in order to win, they have to almost denigrate themselves. They have to make themselves feel ready but inadequate, capable but dissatisfied, or risk losing the sense of urgency that is so critical to inspiration. Having spent their careers angry and unfulfilled, most athletes, if they want to feel happy and satisfied in retirement, must craft a new narrative to justify their lifelong commitment to something so invalidating. This involves reformulating the narrative of their lives, augmenting and deleting when necessary. In other words, it requires the creation of a personal myth.

This new myth, usually romantic and sentimental, is the narrative the former athlete will publicly share moving forward. It's a nostalgia-soaked narrative co-opted by friends and family, who are usually eager to help prop up the player and perhaps have already created myths of their own. The myth is the narrative emeritus the player will use to introduce himself at summer camps to impressionable kids looking for role models. It's the narrative former athletes both fight against and revel in replaying as they go to sleep at night, dreaming of the glory days that may or may not have been all that glorious. It's the narrative they need to believe in order to feel okay about themselves now, away from their sport.

But there are obvious problems with creating myths. The first problem is that it's usually a fragile myth, always threatened by suppressed memories or by a new generation of players who are clearly better. The second problem with the narrative is that as long as the retired athlete yields to it he or she will never be able to die, and therefore never be able to healthily transition away from their sport.

Earlier drafts of this book were mythical testaments to my own narrative. Obsessed with the immortality of my athletic self, I refused to accept, let alone reflect on, the truth of my playing career, and it was only with rewrite after rewrite that I was able to scrape away the myth and stare down my life with a basketball with real honesty. In other words, only by acknowledging the truth, stripped free of self-created myth, was I able to prepare myself to die. What you are reading here, then, is the self-eulogy of my career as an athlete, written many years later than it needed to be.

If I could go back and change one thing about my retirement, I would throw myself a party, a bittersweet funeral in which, alongside friends and family, I would celebrate and mourn my first death, which is to say I would force its arrival. I would order trusted ex-teammates to slap me across the face and shout, "It's over! It's over!," again and again. "There's no going back, you demented son of a bitch!" I'd want them to scream at me, until it sunk in. Then we'd watch clips of my best and worst days on the court, and they'd point at the television and say, "This is exactly what happened. Here's where you succeeded, here's where you failed." Then everyone would hug me and tell me that they loved me no matter what I had or hadn't done on the court. That they still recognized me when I wasn't wearing a uniform. That it was okay that I was uncertain about the future. And that it was okay if I was insecure about who I was without a ball in my hands.

Instead of a party/funeral, however, in the days after my last game I lobbed my feet up on an empty berth in a train chugging east out of Budapest, en route to Romania, where, isolated, I didn't have to think about who I was or what I was transitioning into.

An athlete's prime — that perfect blend of still-young legs

and veteran-savvy mind — is generally considered to fall between twenty-six and thirty years of age. I retired from professional basketball at age twenty-seven, when I was still relatively healthy. Despite all the tweaks and sprains I'd suffered over the years, my body could've help up for several more seasons. Mentally, I'd reached a point where I could see the game more clearly and slowly than ever. After several successful seasons in Europe, I commanded a solid monthly salary, and a few more years of bolstering my bank accounts could've prepared me that much better for rainy days in the future.

Years removed from the game, well-meaning people still ask me why I quit when I did. They'll stare up at me curiously, perhaps pityingly, as if waiting to hear of a genetic disorder or a heart arrhythmia, something unfortunate but understandable. Instead I give them rote answers that I've long practiced on myself. I say I stopped because I didn't want to wear out my body, or I tell of my older teammates, the ones who kept playing into their mid- and late-thirties, who hobbled around and kept painkillers with their wallets and keys. I say I'd rather be healthy and active at fifty than keep playing just to keep playing. Basketball, anyway, by twenty-seven, had become a job, and speaking of jobs, I'll say, I didn't want to be starting a new one, a brand new career back in the States, at thirty-five. If the questioner is still unconvinced, I'll finish by stating it was simply time to hang 'em up; you know when you know.

The practical overtones of these answers fit a certain version of me, but they're also incomplete and perhaps even false. Basketball had often been a job to me, even before I was paid to play, and if anything basketball became less of a job the older I became, when I learned to enjoy the game for the sake of enjoying the game. As for quitting basketball early to avoid starting a new career too late, to that I ask, what career was I planning to start?

I remember a moment when I was sixteen or seventeen. I'm standing by my mailbox in Virginia, holding that day's dose of recruiting letters, picking out the few I'd actually open. They were the usual blurbs, one pitch bleeding into the next. No matter how many I read, I couldn't quite grasp the idea that universities would spend time and energy to lure me in, that they'd pay for me to go to school simply because I was decent at basketball. But I was better than decent. I was tall and had a solid grounding in the fundamentals, a solid basketball IQ, and a soft touch around the rim. So maybe I didn't *want* to believe a school would invest so much in me. I didn't *want* to accept that basketball could become more than the varsity sport it was to me then.

I place the opened letters on top of the unopened ones and trudge back to the house, considering without words, and not for the first time, that I might not want to play basketball beyond high school. The more uncertain I am about this, the more I know I will, as I know I won't have the courage to say no. Too many people have invested too much in my career already for me to turn down a scholarship offer. I feel obligated to all the coaches who tell me I can "make it," who say I have the talent and work ethic to get there. I feel similarly obligated to my height, as if being tall is predestination, and to my ego, which likes the prestige local stardom has already afforded me.

Still holding the letters, I think about the day when I'll be done with it all, a blurry sight arising on the horizon of my mind's eye. It's the vision a soldier might feel on the eve of boot camp, imagining his honorable discharge from the army after several tours of duty many years down the road. I let the feeling linger a moment before dumping the stack of letters into the recycling bin, and then I go do what I perhaps love most at sixteen: I put on some basketball shoes and head out to the driveway to shoot hoops.

Ten or eleven years later, in a dinghy locker room in Hungary, I lived that very moment I'd envisioned as a teenager. I'd done it. I'd survived and made it to the end of my career. But that still didn't explain why I retired at the dawn of my prime. Perhaps my best answer is this: I retired because I felt I'd fulfilled my obligation to the consumerist pressures of the game, had fulfilled the expectations imposed on me by my height, by my talent and ego, by my coaches and teammates. At some point in my youth, basketball had been taken from me, and in its place the authorities handed me a checklist. To prove your worth, you must accomplish the following, they said. By the time I finished my fifth professional year, I had my proof in hand, which meant I was finally okay with quitting.

In other words, retirement wasn't premature anymore; my pedigree was good enough. Four years of Division I basketball at a great mid-major school under a respected coach, five years of professional basketball in reputable European leagues, two All-Star teams, two All-League selections, and a couple of championships. It was collectively good enough to say goodbye. Good enough for the Dean of Expectation to issue a degree. And good enough for me to walk out of that arena in Hungary with no prevailing contract obligations or outside expectations, no more IOUs to the sport in any way whatsoever (or so I thought).

I'd long tried to imagine what my life would be like without basketball. Nearly every scenario was positive, an Eden in which I was free to do whatever I wanted, no longer beholden to the idea of *making it*. But, retired, I was finding that the difficult thing about being free to make life's big decisions is that you have to make them. Retired, I no longer had Mike lining up jobs. There was no obvious next step, like college was after high school and the European leagues were after college, and for the first time in my life I would be paving my own roads, outside of the basketball bubble. I would have to create my own measures of success, my own definition of *making it*, something I'd never before been forced to do.

The most authentic parts of me wanted to travel and read and perhaps write a novel, but I quickly yielded to convention and decided I'd pursue a Masters degree in Environmental Policy in hopes of getting a respectable job. I filled out a number of applications, listing Kondori Liberec, Baloncesto Gijon, and Paks Atomeromu as my previous employers. Next, I listed the skills I'd utilized with each employer, but what practical skills, exactly, had I been making use of in Europe? Shooting threes? Jump hooks?

On paper, my prospects for employment after basketball were perhaps decent. I had a degree from Davidson, spoke a few languages, had played five-plus years of professional basketball in four different countries, and had traveled to big cities and little villages all over the world. I'd have a Master's degree in a year or two, plus I was tall and white. In an initial interview, I could spew all the right teamwork clichés and how they'd overlap in an office.

Put me in a windowless room with an astute company psychologist, however, and let them probe deep within my secret drawers, and I might not have appeared as desirable as my cover letter wanted you to believe. My actual office experience was more or less nonexistent, and as much as 'works well as part of a team' is a desirable trait in an employee, 'shoots the top of the key three consistently' really only fits one brand of resume. 'Lacks long-term career initiative' shouldn't be on any. 'Blindly insecure about his place in the world' and 'still struggling with obsessive-compulsive symptoms' belong on a psychiatric report. I didn't even know how to make coffee.

To boost my resume, I decided to volunteer with two environmental organizations, and my brief tenures with both are noteworthy for the way I interacted with the leaders in each. The first was a grassroots non-profit, Save Our Seine, that tasked itself with taking care of a local river, directed by an older, white-haired guy named Mark. I impressed him in our interview, and he tasked me with researching and writing content for potential use in grants and their quarterly newsletter. He set clear deadlines and expectations and checked in on me regularly, and I knew exactly what he wanted me to do as he set me loose to do it. I completed my research and articles on time and earned Mark's high praise. "If you ever need a job," he told me later, "let me know."

The other organization was a collection of high-up business and professor types, whose goal was shifting energy use in Manitoba away from fossil fuels and into alternative sources. Once again, I impressed in my lunch interview, where I told them I had plenty of free time and plenty of ambition. In response, they offered me plenty of responsibility, which I accepted. Contrary to Mark, their ideas for me were vague and abstract. They gave me a few stray pieces and said build something, granting me the freedom to take the task where I wanted to take it. But, so used to being micromanaged by coaches, where I wanted to go could only mean where *they* wanted to go, and since I didn't really know what they wanted, I had little idea where to take the first step. I could've asked for clarification, but the thought of them thinking I couldn't get it right the first time was too much. As a result, I agonized and fretted about what to do, and ended up not doing much at all.

I played four years of high school ball, four years of college ball, and almost three years of professional basketball before I missed a single game or practice due to an injury. I came down with the flu once and sat out a game or two, but I'd never been seriously hurt. "Just get loose," was my long-running response to physical pain, and for over a decade I employed it to good measure, hobbling around in warm-ups until the blood started flowing and the pain went away.

Far worse than the physical pain associated with an injury is the mental anguish that coagulates around it, a wave of misery that often mimics Elizabeth Kubler Ross's five stages of death: denial, anger, bargaining, depression, acceptance. Analogizing athletic injury with death is perhaps a touch extreme, but not totally inaccurate, as athletes who identify solely with their sport are, when injured and unable to compete, not really alive. At the end of my third season in Paks, I sprained the AC joint in my shoulder, and in my fourth and fifth seasons I bruised my ribs and twisted my ankle, respectively. In the brief rehabilitory stints I endured for each injury, I took care of my body, icing and massaging as needed. When a doctor asked me to rate my pain on a scale of 1 to 10, I had no problem providing an accurate number. I did this so I could return to the court as quickly as possible, so I could feel alive again. Playing through physical pain was often encouraged in my career, but it was not considered a weakness to *feel* pain or want to heal.

But what about the injuries that nobody could see, the injuries that don't turn black and blue and don't show up on X-rays?

Some months after I retired from basketball, at the recommendation of my therapist, I consulted a psychiatrist and for the first time in my life received an official medical diagnosis of the obsessive-compulsive mindset I'd lived with since I was at least nine years old.

Treatment options for OCD continue to evolve, but no treatment can ever be consummated without a demand from the sufferer to be treated. This involves the sufferer stepping forward and admitting they're suffering, and perhaps there is no professional arena where admitting a need for (mental) treatment is more frowned upon than in sports. From a young age, emotionally injured players (nearly all of us) are taught to say, "I'm good," and to not even recognize their pain.

When the 2011-12 basketball season began, my name wasn't on any roster, but Emma had accepted a contract to play volleyball in Sweden, and so I followed her there. My parents worried that I was mothballing major life decisions, that I was, more or less, wasting my time. But to me following Emma to Europe would allow me to keep taking baby steps as I continued to find myself anew.

Emma and I settled into a functional little apartment in a tiny town outside Malmo, just across the Oresund from

Denmark. She went to practice everyday, and I, well, didn't. Intent on learning the language, I combed through daily editions of *Expressen*, Sweden's version of the *New York Post*, becoming exceptionally knowledgeable of national murders, rapes, and celebrity gossip, topics I invariably introduced into conversation whenever Emma and I found ourselves being social with Swedes.

My proficiency in criminal vocabulary was perhaps amusing, but it was also enough for Emma's team, short on cash, to offer me the job of PA announcer/emcee at home games, my first real job after basketball. This meant I sat courtside, mic in hand, and read off the starting lineups, substitutions, and scores. At first I was quite formal, but after a game or two I became increasingly ballsy, quoting *Braveheart* and *Gladiator* monologues during time-outs, calling out players from the other team, and rapping Kanye West verses between sets.

Still talking to the therapist in Charlottesville once a week, I made good on my vow to keep taking steps. Everyday viscerally aroused some unexplored episode of my life, like the time in Gijon when I refused to hold a teammate's infant baby for fear that I would throw the baby off a balcony; or like in Norrkoping when, returning home from a club in the early morning with a couple of my teammates, I abruptly opened the moving taxi's door and jumped out; or like the time at Davidson when, after losing an erection during sex, and in what I didn't know at the time was a not-uncommon symptom of OCD, I was briefly convinced I was gay.

It was onerous and grueling to review the tape of my life each week — you have to feel to heal, and there was so much to feel. It was also a humbling process, as it

158

indirectly revealed how blind and insensitive I'd long been on so many subjects.

Take race. I played for two AAU basketball teams growing up. One of these teams was composed solely of white players, and for tournaments in distant cities we traveled with our families in a cruise-controlled caravan, stayed in nice hotels, and ate out in decent restaurants. My other team was often all African-American, coaches included, except for me, and on road trips we survived on fast food and gas station gummy bears, and when we weren't driving all night we stayed five to a room in budget hotels. My nickname on this all-black team was "Snow," which prompted my mother to ask my AAU coach why they called me that. The coach smiled and said it was because my shot was as soft as falling snow.

On road trips with my all-black team, I didn't immediately understand why hotel clerks, gas station attendants, and waitresses at restaurants often treated us with such cold reserve. In Maryland, once, a hotel manager refused outright to book us rooms, to which I didn't consciously compute, *It's because those guys are black.* Other times, when we had to interact with a white face, the coaches would say things like, "You go up there and ask, Snow," and for years I assumed they sent me on these little errands because I was the most responsible. I didn't understand why the occupants of our team van would noticeably tense whenever we passed a cop car, or the way everyone would stop talking and stare straight ahead when we strolled by an officer in a mall.

We took these trips before smartphones assaulted our culture, so our van rides were often boisterous, Gatorade-fueled debate sessions, and as our conversations unfolded it often surprised me how funny, self-aware, and culturally perceptive my black teammates were. I felt annoyed because as the white guy I wanted to be, and assumed I should've been, the smartest and most with-it guy on the team. If these guys had thick accents and a vocabulary much more limited than mine, how were they making funnier, wittier points?

One morning, my junior year, I took a multiple-choice exam sitting next to an African-American teammate. While I cruised through the questions, he spent time filling in the bubbles so that they spelled "FUCK THIS." I attended first-rate public schools in upper middle-class neighborhoods, but none addressed how hundreds of years of brutally oppressive American history, and its fictive overtones, might've created that dichotomy between that teammate and me. In high school history class, the Middle Passage and the Trail of Tears garnered a glossed-over paragraph or two, total, and Colonialism was presented like a game of *Risk*. My junior year American History textbook contained a blurb on Jim Crow, but after reading it I was confused as to whether he was a person or a law, to say nothing of the era's reverberating impact. American history in white schools somehow pulls off the feat of mentioning the oppressed without acknowledging the oppressors. I was a white American male educated in white American schools. How much did I really know? I'd been teammates, roommates, and colleagues with so many African-Americans over the years. How many had I ever really known?

Then there was sex. One summer one of my AAU teams flew out to Las Vegas for a tournament. We stayed at Circus Circus, the big top-inspired hotel at the far northern end of the strip, and a few of the guys thought it'd be fun to pool their money and call up an escort service. When the escort arrived, most everyone freaked and bolted the room, leaving me alone with the woman, who was light-skinned and pleasant-looking. I was a virgin then, somewhat afraid of sex, and still under the assumption that hooking up with a girl demanded the complex and precise execution of a scripted sequence of lines and behaviors. That all this woman required to allow penetration was a few sweat-stained twenties unrolled from my palm was painfully incongruent. Not that I would've really known what to do anyway, as I'd largely learned about sex through literary metaphors in books. The real life stuff — the smells and the insecurities, the stickiness and fear, the ungovernable eruptions both somatic and of the heart — in other words, all the less romantic practical stuff that accompanies getting naked with someone else — I had no idea.

All my confusion and inexperience kind of coalesced in that moment alone with the woman. She could've given me a solid anatomical lesson on sex and have been the least judgmental about it, but at the same time, her mere presence and the professional objectification of her body were, perhaps a little ironically, a very visceral indication of how much I had to learn about love and intimate self-expression. Together we sat for several long minutes — me on the bed, her standing by the door — until she realized that I wasn't going to give her any business and that the other guys probably weren't coming back anytime soon, at which point she shouldered her tiny little purse and left.

Growing up, I was a cog in a system I didn't understand, and I was afraid to question my cogness. I often didn't even know that I *should* be questioning my cogness. But, in Sweden, I was finally untangling.

One day, not long after her season ended (and, alas, my gig as PA announcer), Emma and I took a walk, the sad kind where we didn't walk back together.

"I don't even know you anymore," she told me. Depressing as it was, her saying this was the most curiously marvelous thing.

Chapter 8 — Rebirth

For the first thirty or so years that basketball was played, there was no such thing as post play. In fact, many leagues instituted a rule preventing players from keeping their backs to the basket for longer than three seconds. There were no jump shots back then, either, just flat-footed two-handed flings towards the hoop, often with a single leg kicking backwards as a follow-through. Similar to soccer or hockey today, basketball's positions were once more geographical, with "forwards" advancing to the basket and looking to score, while "guards" hung back and defended. Until 1922, traveling was considered a foul. Until 1945, players who subbed out couldn't re-enter the game, and until 1949, coaches weren't allowed to coach during games, not even during timeouts; they could only address their teams at halftime. Even out-of-bounds wasn't always out of bounds; until 1915, the first player to touch the ball after it crossed a baseline or sideline was allowed to throw it in, which prompted dangerous rushes into the crowd to snag that first touch. (Many games were played in gyms featuring an elevated track, when the ball bounced up there teams were known to forego the steps and instead gymnastically heave a player up over the railing.) The balls in those early eras contained an inflatable bladder which needed to be filled with air before games, often at a gas station. Even the media photos of basketball's incipience seem strange, the players looking less like athletes than muscular versions of C-3PO holding a ball.

Throughout the 1920s and 1930s basketball fielded numerous professional leagues, often played wherever managers and promoters could find a playing surface that could conceivably pass as a court — in casinos, for instance, or tiny dance halls with slick floors, or in church basements with 9-foot ceilings supported by immovable steel poles shooting up from the ground like extra screeners. The game was heterogeneous, subject to the whims of the many regions and arenas in which it was played, with no set dimensions for a court, no agreed upon collection of concrete rules, and sometimes no way of telling what was basketball and what wasn't.

Recognizing the disarray, basketball's governing bodies sought to instill some order. In 1929, the National Association of Basketball Coaches (the NABC, which still exists today) met in New York to determine once and for all the fate of the dribble, which since basketball's inception had been under attack by conservatives who deemed it unnecessary and plodding. Naismith's original rules said nothing about dribbling. Among the early variations of basketball was a style wherein the player with the ball could toss it up in the air and then run and catch it, like a self-pass, advancing closer to the basket. Other leagues limited the number of dribbles to one or three, and some banned it altogether. At that meeting, the NABC voted 9-8 to permanently eliminate the dribble, then an hour later voted again and reversed their decision, setting basketball on a new course.

In 1937, basketball's governing officials initiated a similarly historic move. For the game's first half-century, players for both teams trudged back to half court for a jump ball after every made basket. The clock continued to run while this happened, which meant a good ten minutes or so of gameplay was actually spent setting up the resumption of play. The frequent tip-offs artificially elevated the importance of the center, who in those early days could get away with limiting himself to grabbing rebounds and winning all the taps. Games were slow and bumbly and often excessively rough. To fix this, players were now allowed to inbound the ball behind the baselines immediately following a basket. Because of this new rule, the pace of play rightfully accelerated, fast breaks and full-court presses developed, and scoring averages dramatically increased.

Along with the rule changes, several other stimuli helped homogenize and popularize the game. The first came from Ned Irish, a New York City newspaperman whose assignments in the early 1930s included coverage of the relatively underappreciated college basketball circuit. Recognizing both the quality of play and the passion college teams generated in their hometowns, he convinced Madison Square Garden bigwigs to stage a series of doubleheaders featuring the best college teams from coast to coast (a doubleheader was needed, it was said, because a single game wasn't yet worth it to fans, particularly before the rules changes mentioned above).

In December 1936, Stanford, a west coast power very few on the east coast had ever seen play, squared off in MSG against local favorite Long Island University. Long Island University was coached by Clair Bee, a future Hall of Famer who, among other accomplishments, introduced the 1-3-1 defense and helped institute the 3-second rule in the lane. Stanford's best player was Hank Luisetti, who en route to a game-high 15 points (in a low-scoring 45-31 loss) showed off on basketball's biggest stage the beta version of the one-handed jump shot, the evolution of the flat-footed two-handed set shot which was still standard at the time. He wasn't the first to use it in a game (to avoid compressing the chest, women had been advised to shoot one-handed for decades), but he was the first male to employ it in the Garden in front of the masses. The media and fans in attendance wrote and gossiped about the jump shot's success, cementing both the Luisetti legend and a new era of play.

The doubleheaders were popular enough for Irish and his pals to organize a national year-end tournament to declare a single collegiate champion, which is how the National Invitation Tournament (NIT) was born in 1938. Not to be outdone, the NCAA quickly followed with their own national tournament in 1939, although with a different format — a region-based gig that was the precursor to today's March Madness.

World War II was another homogenizer for the sport. Although the need for soldiers depleted rosters, the game remained popular on military bases, where players from different parts of the country were forced to play together and thus adapt to different playing styles. Similarly, the men who weren't drafted were forced to combine teams and leagues, further spreading and streamlining styles of play.

After the war, the U.S. population, having largely shaken the slump of the Great Depression, was flush with cash and free time and looking for ways to spend it, which is why every sports league, including the nascent Basketball Association of America (BAA), saw record attendance in the post-war years. In 1949, the BAA and the National Basketball League merged to form the NBA, and despite a turbulent first few decades in which the league battled racism, drug use, violence, lawsuits and the American Basketball Association (ABA), the league survived to welcome the arrival of Larry Bird and Magic Johnson in 1980, the year basketball historians often refer to as the birth of the modern NBA.

The genesis of my personal modern era, the dawn of my life after basketball, began, of all places, in a tiny village snug in the Himalayas of India. After leaving Sweden, I returned to Charlottesville, where I hoped to put my master's degree to good use. Instead, I found myself stocking shelves at a local Whole Foods, the first time I'd ever really earned money without a basketball in my hands. It wasn't awful by any means, but by the end of my first shift I was already dreaming about what would come next: travel. I wasn't ready to stop moving. I had to get away again. I called my friend Dana, who at the time was, like me, somewhat lost and confused, and I asked her if she wanted to go see the world.

"Where are we going?" she asked.

"Not sure," I responded. "I guess we need to look at a map."

I pulled out my old map, the one on which I'd stared at Gijon and Liberec so long ago, and Dana and I began plotting our trip.

In mid-June 2013, we left for India on one-way tickets. Our hotel in Paharganj, Delhi's backpacker haunt, was owned by Manpreet, an elderly man with a spotless turban who sat regally behind the front desk and jotted our information in a colossal logbook that looked like it belonged in an antiquity museum. Next to the desk lay a bare mattress on which two waiflike men slept side by side in street clothes, a couple pairs of worn rubber flip-flops lined up along its edge.

When Manpreet finished writing he rose and led us to our room, which was austere yet clean. "Water is no good," he said, pointing at the sink and waving a finger. "No drinking," he warned, and with a side-to-side squiggle of his head, he bid us goodnight.

Some hours later I awoke to go to the bathroom, where, out of habit, I bent over the sink, stuck my mouth under the faucet and drank deeply.

The next morning, after a breakfast of overripe papaya, eggs and toast (my stomach, miraculously, stayed sane), Dana and I maneuvered down the main thoroughfare of Paharganj, around shopkeepers pouring water on their stoops to keep down the dust, past vendors selling fly-besieged apricots and almonds and marjoram, and past donkey-drawn carriages and emaciated stray dogs. We passed under advertisements that jutted into the road like elbows from a car window — Hotel All Iz Well, Hotel Kwality, Hotel Krishna Cottage. Cries of "Lambo!" mysteriously erupted in my direction, as did assertions that I was from Holland. I could smell urine, cumin, hibiscus, perspiration, and exhaust. The sun was a love god, its heat a sweltering hug, and there was no wriggling out. At the end of the Main Bazar, we climbed into the back of a mechanized, hollowed out green tooth, politely known as an autorickshaw, and zipped back to our hotel already exhausted.

Tourists in India have plenty to do in Delhi — Connaught Place, Red Fort, India Gate — and can similarly keep themselves occupied in the northern city of Shimla, where the English escaped the brutal summers during the Raj, but the drive from Delhi to Shimla deserves scrutiny all on its own. The first few hours lapse into an attempt to merely exit Delhi gridlock: functioning traffic lights cycling their colors to a blind audience; traffic officers shouting and blowing whistles in the middle of intersections, similarly ignored; the window of a bus abruptly shattering and falling to the pavement below like a broken wave simmering on shore; a man thrown off his motorbike, the contents of his bag scattering into traffic; the child pawns of the homeless mafia jumping from window to window, jabbing their foreheads repeatedly with all five fingers, as if trying to pluck a stubborn bindi; slightly more affluent waresmen in the synapses of traffic lanes selling jalebis and samosas; a line of men on the curb waiting to get haircuts; all of it chaos and stagnation, yet somehow a functioning system.

Dana had insisted that we pepper our travels with bursts of volunteering, as if to justify all the time we were taking for ourselves, and in India she'd chosen the Wahoe Foundation, a non-governmental organization (NGO) founded by a sage and quirky man named Gurvinder. When Dana and I first met him, he wasted no time describing our auras, analyzing our moles, and opining that our chakras needed balancing. There was a small village in the Himalayas, he added, a day's bus ride from Shimla, that could use English-speaking volunteers.

So it was with Gurvinder that Dana and I made our way to Shimla, along with our driver and another volunteer. In early afternoon the bustle of Delhi opened up into dusty Punjabi flatlands, at the far end of which began the Himalayas. In late afternoon the road grew serpentine, the car hissy, its passengers cramped and bored. At dusk we stopped for chai at a small roadside hut manned by at least six men idling around a clay stove, our tea served steaming and sweet in dented tin cups. By nightfall, feeling like a kid, I couldn't help asking Gurvinder how much further we had to go.

"Oh, we're here," he said, gesturing out the window at the layers of lights sloping up the mountainside. "This is Shimla."

Dana and I both leaned over to check out the view.

"Shimla is apparently where Rudyard Kipling got the inspiration to write *The Jungle Book*," Dana said.

I nodded. I could see why. Like Cinque Terre in Italy, most of the city was vertical, only much higher up. Most people look up at the clouds. In Shimla, you lived in them.

As stunning as Shimla was, it was not our final destination, and so the next morning Dana and I boarded a local bus for Siri Village, where we were due as volunteers. The bus was full but eerily silent. Gurvinder and the other volunteer were headed elsewhere, and Dana and I were now on our own. We had our bags, plus gifts and supplies for the village, but there wasn't nearly enough rack space for all our stuff. Because the bus was sold out, I assumed we'd be letting people off along the way, freeing up some room, but at every stop — a wave from the side of the road earned you a stop — more people boarded until the entire affair felt like one of those radio station gimmicks where they try to fit as many people as possible into a tiny space.

I couldn't tell what aggravated me more, the suffocating presence of people or the quality of the roads. The bus itself was stiff and utilitarian, like a vehicular erection that had been prematurely yanked from a Soviet assembly line. It grunted and roared up inclines and wheezed and screeched its way down declines. Out the windows to the right I could see the stone face of the towering mountains we were trying to navigate; to the left sweeping panoramas dive-bombed across the low Himalayas, views that in another circumstance I might've described as breathtaking if my breath wasn't already deprived by the high elevation and lack of oxygen.

Passengers elbowed for room, argued for fun, and leaned wholesale as the bus turned, like the crew in the slow-motion van going off the bridge in *Inception*. I closed my eyes and watched the fire burn on the backs of my lids, anticipating the moment when we'd slip off the edge, wondering what those few seconds before death would feel like. Several times I silently called out for my mother.

Every so often we'd pass a town, a line of ramshackle buildings lining the road, and just as quickly the town would disappear. Footpaths snaked their way up into the surrounding foliage, and makeshift Hindu shrines, spaced every mile or so along the road, infused the landscape with mysticism. In mid-afternoon, after eight hours on the bus, we arrived at a jumble of open-air dwellings, still not Siri, just the closest town. There were no signs we could read, so we had to take the ticket-wallah on faith that we were in the right spot, and the right spot meant being met by the right person, Kehar, a young man from Siri who was supposed to hike down from the village to pick us up.

If Kehar was there, we couldn't see him, and Dana and I were hard to miss. We stood next to crates of bottled water and orange soda and waited, magnetizing eyes and attracting a crowd of disquisitive men. I tried to keep my face neutral, as if I knew exactly where I was and what I was doing, but the clustering men talked in increasingly animated tones, gesturing towards us and pointing at our bags and boxes as if we were an exhibition.

The circle kept getting smaller, the gesturing men closer, and the ruckus louder. Five minutes became ten, and ten, twenty, until finally a man broke the circumference and walked right up to us. "Yan?"

"Kehar?"

After proper introductions and apologies were made, the crowd dispersed and Kehar walked us to an idling jeep operated by one of his buddies, who zipped us twenty minutes along a river to a trailhead. The jeep zoomed off, and then it was just Dana, Kehar, and me in what was suddenly the quietest place in India. For the first time in weeks I could hear the sounds of nature, pure and unmuted. Not used to the silence, my head roared.

From the trailhead we started up a rutted path, the air getting clearer and the scenery more beautifully surreal with every switchback. When we stopped to rest, Dana slung her pack off her shoulders, plopped down on a big rock, and suggested turning back. Her suggestion was instantly a metaphor for all the progress I'd made since I'd retired from basketball. "You know you don't mean that," I told her.

Dana assured me she did, relaying her thoughts to me in no uncertain terms. "The only thing that's stopping me is the thought of having to get back on that bus," she said, wiping hair from her eyes.

I glanced at Kehar to see if he was catching on. He carried

a black umbrella to shield himself against the sun, and was twirling it now like Mary Poppins.

"We can do this," I kept telling Dana after we set off again, until Dana told me to shut up, and then I repeated the phrase to myself.

It was dusk when we reached the village, which turned out to be not much of a village at all, just a few small shacks/houses lined up one-two-three on a peninsular slope jutting out from a steep incline. The hillside around the village fell off sharply into patches of tomato plants, which gave way to brush leading all the way down to a river roaring with monsoon excess. The path continued on the far side, weaving around the mountain en route to more distant villages.

Dana and I weren't in Kansas anymore, but neither were the villagers, in a way, as they were descendants of the so-called Untouchable caste who had generations ago fled their lives in urban areas to start over in a place where nobody would bother them. Several had gathered to greet us. Mumta, seventeen, was studying in Delhi at the time but had come home for a couple weeks to help translate for Dana and me. Mumta's mother, Mumma, had lost her husband when he'd fallen off a cliff face some years before. Prakash, a young cousin of Mumta's, greeted me with a "Hello meestah!" and Kalpana, an undersized and possibly malnourished girl of four or five who lived next door, parroted whatever Prakash said.

We exchanged Namaste's, igniting the chorus of introductory half-sentences and funky gestures you get when not everyone speaks the same language. Mumta proceeded to give Dana and me a brief tour, leading us into a roofless structure, no bigger than a walk-in closet, with a holed out muddy mound in the center. "So this must be the bathroom," I said.

"No, this is the winter kitchen," Mumta replied.

After the tour, it was time for the women to make dinner in the summer kitchen, which was the front stoop. Mumta poured lentils into a pan and sifted through them, removing tiny pebbles and sticks, while Mumma attended to an iron pot that hung over a small fire. Red onions no bigger than ping pong balls were chopped up and tossed in, then a clove of garlic, radishes, and heaping spoonfuls of dark spices. Prakash and Kalpana ran around, showing off and asking questions: "You, meestah, berf-day?"

To eat, we sat cross-legged on small mats circled around a candle while Prakash filled our tin cups with sour lassi served from a wooden jug. I made a scooping motion as he passed, and he darted over to a crate from which he extracted two spoons, wiping them on his shirt before handing them to Dana and me.

The next morning I awoke to find Prakash standing at the foot of my sleeping mat, grinning. It was unclear how long he'd been standing there. "Chai?" he chirped.

"Yes, please," I said, rubbing my eyes and sitting up.

"Okee," he said, "I go milk dee goat."

All around Siri, mountain peaks heaved upwards like giant crooked teeth. One afternoon, I watched from afar as groups of Indians crested the high-altitude horizons and made their way single-file down the mountainside trails, drumming slow patterns on instruments hung around their necks, and chanting low and ominous-sounding intonations. They were arriving for a party at a house across the valley. Everyone was invited, including Dana and me. Mumta led us over around six, although I can't be sure of the time because I had stopped wearing a watch. Like everyone else in Siri, I'd begun to go as the sun went.

Dinner was lentils, chapati, and rice, the same meal we ate everyday, but scooped a little thicker and piled a little higher than normal. After eating, Dana and I hung out with a gaggle of Indian teenagers, most of whom were cousins or second cousins. Many had spent all day walking to the village, Mumta said, and they'd party all night and then walk home all day the next day. I convinced them to sing Dana and me an Indian song, and then I insisted I sing them an American song in return, rapping Kanye West's verse from "Clique" before easing into Katy Perry's "Teenage Dream."

A little later the men gathered indoors for a "meditation." We sat in a room empty save for a mound of charcoal flanked by a pile of wheat berries and a rack of iron weaponry — two swords, an ax, and a maul. One of the men lit a small stick of incense, attached it to a black chain and then, like a priest with a thurible, waved it back and forth over the berries and weapons while the rest of the room prayed for good health and harvests.

Dana and I would give a number of English lessons throughout our stay, and our cultural exchanges went far beyond Kanye West and Katy Perry. In addition, I quietly tasked myself with another, more personal duty. One dusky evening, as the men sat around waiting for the women to finish cooking dinner, I birthed a basketball from my bag. It was bright yellow and rough, the outdoor kind that makes your fingers feel prickly when you dribble it, and the only one I could find in Shimla. Feeling a little like a missionary, I presented the ball to Prakash, who accepted it, fingered it, then stared at me puzzlingly. He tossed it to Kehar, who held it dubiously, then started juggling it like a soccer ball. Grinning, Kehar kicked it back to Prakash, who attempted the same.

As encouragingly as I could, I gathered Prakash and Kalpana in the patch of dirt behind the house and showed them how to dribble. I twisted some wire into a rim and tried to demonstrate shooting. I showed them a defensive stance. "When I clap my hands, you slap the ground and yell 'Defense!,'" I bellowed.

While both were mildly coordinated in a I'm-growing-up-in-the-Himalayas kind of way, neither Prakash nor Kalpana had much hope of "making it" in any traditional sense, and yet both were looking up at me with wild eyes, happy that I was taking an interest in them, happy that they were learning this American game. I couldn't match their happiness, however, as their lack of potential made me feel like teaching them anything would be pointless.

Prakash was nine or ten years old when I visited Siri, around the age I was when I first began to take basketball seriously, when the game first began to *matter*. I was nine or ten when I first realized that basketball could boost my self-esteem, could help me make friends, and help me impress girls. Basketball had given structure to my life when my life might have otherwise been unbearably chaotic, and the sport was a daily dose of familiarity in a world of frequent uncertainty. In short, basketball had kept me from succumbing to the temptations and substances that sucked the lives and livelihoods of far too many people I knew growing up.

Over my twenty years in the game, basketball had given me opportunities to live in foreign countries while making money, opportunities to push myself way past ridiculous mental and physical boundaries, and opportunities to perform in ways most people never get the chance to perform. But for all the opportunities basketball had provided, for all the stability and structure it had given me, I had to give basketball something in return, namely, *me*.

But basketball didn't seem to matter to Prakash — he couldn't even recognize a ball. My relationship with the game didn't matter to him, but it somehow mattered to me that it didn't matter to him, because, if basketball didn't matter to him, then *I* didn't matter to him.

It's said that every athlete dies twice, once when he quits playing and once for real. It was in Siri Village, as far away from a basketball court as I've ever been, that it finally registered that I would have to find a way to let the sport go, completely, at least for a while, and rebuild myself anew, or else I'd never find peace away from the sport. When I left Siri the basketball had tumbled off a bluff, where it lay hidden in some shrubs. Nobody seemed particularly eager to retrieve it.

There's some debate as to when and how sports first developed, but a predominant theory asserts that sports began as a way for militaries to determine who was and was not fit for combat, with team sports mimicking a battle between armies and individual sports representing mano-a-mano engagements.

The Mesoamerican ballgame, a game which goes by many

names (we'll go with pitz), was played as early as 1400 BCE in pre-Columbian Mexico and as far south as modern day Nicaragua. The details of pitz varied over time and region, but it was generally played with a rubber ball on a long court boxed in by slanted stone walls, with the primary object being to keep the ball in play without using the arms. Points were scored when one team hit the opposing team's far wall, or by passing the ball through any number of vertical stone rings that lined the sides of the court.

In 2007, while in Honduras, I visited one of these ancient ball courts at the Mayan ruins of Copan, where our tour guide explained that in certain regions the captain of the "winning" team would be rewarded with the literal loss of his head, on the assumption that the victor was best suited to fight the evils lurking in the underworld.

Today, playing fields have evolved, the equipment is different, and the players are paid more, but in some ways not much has changed since the dawn of sports. Although no one earns a pitz-like beheading anymore, it's not apocryphal to say that simply trying to compete in sports requires sacrificing a great deal of who you are.

I sometimes think that the moment I actually retired from basketball was the year — let's call it my sophomore year of high school — when basketball stopped being a game and started being a ruthless god. I *loved* basketball growing up, and in an unfortunate irony, I loved it less the better I became.

Sophomore year was the year I started getting recruited, the year I joined serious AAU teams, and the year newspapers started writing about me. It was the year people began to tell me I could "make it."

That was 2001. Almost twenty years later, as the game has grown and gotten richer, the pressure that was once reserved for the very best has seeped down the line, and now anonymous elementary schoolers live like top-level high schoolers lived barely a generation ago.

Basketball is the only major sport that can trace its origin back to a single man. While Dr. James Naismith is revered today for the game he gave us, it's debatable, and probably unlikely, that he'd appreciate the directions in which the game's many administrative stewards have taken it, namely, by taking his game and turning it into a matter of life and death.

For stewards like myself, whose lives are or were once defined by the game, it can be disconcerting to trace a line back to Naismith's brain on that day in December 1891, when the game was an unrefined recreational idea, to today, when the sport is more easily described on ontological grounds. Naismith, in a way, sits at the top of the basketball family tree, and for those of us who roost in the tree's contemporary branches and who want to honor his legacy while still embracing change, there's a sort of uneasiness that arises when you stare too hard into his long-dead eyes.

In his autobiography, reflecting on the game forty years after he invented it, Naismith wrote "the technique and expertness with which the game is now played are indeed wonderful to me," and it's hard not to see him admiring the handles of Kyrie Irving, the step-back of James Harden, or the dexterity of Anthony Davis. But elsewhere in his life Naismith seemed to give several disapproving nods to the game's progression. In the 1930s, when rule changes streamlined the game, Naismith, as an honorary member of several rules committees, did not support them, even speaking up against the existential 1937 amendment that axed the necessity of a jump ball after every basket. More than that, Naismith never wavered in his belief that basketball should be played more or less exclusively for fun, exercise, and character-building, certainly not for money. Here's Naismith in his autobiography again: "I realize...the amount of good we can do through our athletics and physical education. It is only natural that I should spend much time in determining just what part basketball is playing in this program. The decisions that I have reached in regard to the game are that it is not now and it was never intended to be a complete system of physical education. The main purpose of the game is recreation and the development of certain attributes that are peculiar to the game."

Like with music or science or any other enduring cultural phenomenon, it's antithetical to progress to try to hold on to basketball's theoretical origins. Mozart was Mozart, but without a shift in gears we would've never gotten the blues, and without the blues we would've never gotten the Beatles.

Art evolves, and while some patrons might prefer a Botticelli to a Picasso, and a Picasso to whatever's most current at the Whitney, to interfere with the evolution of art is to wish for it to be dead. Giannis Antetokounmpo, the Milwaukee Bucks' limby "Greek Freak," is not Elgin Baylor, the L.A. Laker great whose artful innovations in the 1960s rewrote the game. Elgin Baylor, in turn, is not Hank Luisetti, the pioneer of the jump shot, and Hank Luisetti is not William Chase, the player who scored basketball's first bucket way back in 1891.

Given the depth and breadth to which basketball has infiltrated popular culture, it's futile to try to define what basketball *should* universally be. Consider the following from Pete Axthelm's *The City Game*, written in 1970 about basketball in poverty-stricken ghettos: "The game is simple, an act of one man challenging another, twisting, feinting, then perhaps breaking free to lean upward, directing a ball toward a target, a metal hoop ten feet above the ground. And a one-on-one challenge takes on wider meaning, defining identity and manhood in an urban society that breeds invisibility."

Or take this from Pat Summitt, Tennessee's legendary women's head coach: "I remember standing on a medal podium at the 1976 Montreal Olympics, imbued with a sense that if you won enough basketball games, there was no such thing as poor, backward, country, female, or inferior."

What basketball means to you is not what it means to me, and what it means to me is not what it means to Maya Moore or Stephon Marbury or Jeff Van Gundy. Basketball is art, with seemingly endless means of composition, presentation, and elucidation. Perhaps since the first day basketball was played, when Naismith's students lost teeth and knocked each other unconscious fighting for the ball, the game surrendered the simplistic intentions of its originator. Like an untrampled field of snow, it was holy only until it became human.

In the same way that no two games are ever exactly alike, the idea of basketball itself can and should be open to constant and ephemeral interpretation by its many honest proprietors. In 1944, in a locked, spectator-free gym in Durham, North Carolina, an all-black team from the North

Carolina College for Negroes defied state law and illegally played an all-white team from Duke Medical School, the first racially integrated game in the American south; the game was a bridge. The NBA's Basketball Without Borders program operates in tens of countries around the world, building athletic foundations and identifying global talent; the game is an architect. In January 2014, at the bequest of Dennis Rodman, several former NBA players traveled to North Korea to play in what they thought would be a diplomatic exhibition, but the exhibition ended up being a birthday present to Supreme Leader Kim Jong-Un; the game was quirky showmanship. On syndicated talk radio NBA old-timers disparage the way basketball is played today; the game is a threat. On playgrounds from Maine to Macau children imagine themselves playing in the NBA; the game is a dream. Elsewhere, the game is a profession, a spectacle, and a proxy for the evolutionary instincts we no longer need. But giving basketball the freedom and space to evolve is not the same as accepting the infrastructure that has developed around it, and basketball in the 21st century, from cutthroat AAU programs for six year olds to overzealous coaches who demand "everything you have," is far too largely structured around money, unresolved intentions, and an obsession with the future.

Returning from India, I moved to Pittsburgh. I found a place in the East End, just a couple of miles from where I was born. My apartment was a tiny studio with a slanted floor; everything was lopsided, so much so that when I cooked on the stove I had to stir constantly lest all the liquid slouch to one side of the pan. The ceilings leaked dust anytime I opened or closed a door or cupboard, and my only furniture was a card table and a fold-out chair. There wasn't enough room for a bed, so I slept on a little air mattress, my legs hanging off at the knees, and when that deflated I spent the next 18 months sleeping on the floor, nightly donning an old pair of padded compression shorts to protect my hips. This wasn't out of poverty; I'd saved well. The run-down apartment felt like all I could take care of, a reflection of how I saw myself at the time. In the studio's closet my framed *Sports Illustrated* cover angled behind several empty suitcases. In another telling sign of my mindset then, it was my souvenirs from travel, items that had nothing to do with basketball, that I chose to display.

That winter I went on a date with a woman who'd also recently returned to Pittsburgh after years away from the city. I wasn't exactly ready for a healthy relationship, but I was scared to be on my own. It felt weird to sit across from someone I couldn't reminisce about India with, but the date went well, and returning home afterwards I did what millennials do when they want to get to know somebody better: I Googled her. Her search results were impressive, my eyebrows stretching a little with every click. When I was done I closed my computer, crossed my arms, and compared her professional resume to my own, as if this was the only way to determine if we were a good match. I felt inferior, and therefore intimidated, when I considered that my basketball pedigree wasn't as "good" as the things I learned about her on the internet. Somehow this mattered.

We saw each other again, and at the end of our second date she climbed up on a curb so we could more easily share our first kiss. When she stepped down she smiled and said, "For the record, I really like your height."

A few days later she came over for dinner, forcing me to

make a Target run to pick up another folding chair. I didn't have a couch, so after eating we sat on the sloped floor and listened to a couple of squirrels scurrying over my ceiling tiles. In certain ways the relationship grew to be rather wonderful; we were on the same page in some subtly crucial way, and she would tell me later that when she returned home after our first date she'd looked at herself in the mirror and told herself that everything was going to change. This turned out to be true, everything did change, but probably not in the way she'd imagined. For no matter how wonderful our relationship seemed, it often felt like I had to act a certain way around her. A *perfect* way. Or at the very least better than every other man aged twenty-four to forty-two, or I'd be kicked to the very same curb she'd first kissed me on. Insecure of who I was, and intimidated by all *she* was, I had to constrict myself to a version of myself that I thought she'd most like, namely, the ghost of an ex-professional basketball player.

Our relationship barely lasted a few months. The day of my thirtieth birthday, she took me to a little restaurant where we answered questions from a stack of conversation-starter cards that sat in ashtrays at each table, and afterwards we took a stroll through the pleasant spring air in one of Pittsburgh's nicer neighborhoods. Everything very right, which was perhaps the reason why I felt the need to make everything very wrong. On the way back to her place, out of the blue, I told her that it had to end. She didn't understand, and I didn't consciously understand my sudden decision either, which made it all the worse because I couldn't give her any sort of legitimate reasoning.

Back at her place, she pounded on my chest and told me I was scared of the good things in my life, that to leave her would be cowardly and that I would regret it. I'd done so much work in therapy, had let go of so much to do with OCD and basketball, but I still wasn't ready to rejoin the world at large, especially with a member of the opposite sex. I walked away from her house expecting to feel relieved, as relief is what I almost always felt after a breakup, but this time there was only shame and deadness and an overwhelming sense of reluctance for the road ahead.

In the fall of 1978, while at Georgia State University, psychologists Pauline Rose Clance and Suzanne Imes published a paper on the "imposter phenomenon" in high-achieving women. These were women who, despite ample evidence to the contrary, felt like they had somehow duped their superiors and colleagues into thinking that they were much brighter than they really were.

"Obviously I'm in this position [of power and success] because my abilities have been overestimated," a participant in Clance and Imes' study reports. "Some mistake was made in the selection process," says another.

The experience of feeling fraudulent and falsely unqualified for success, known popularly today as "imposter syndrome," has since been revealed to affect men as much as women, and has been documented in politics and sports and parenting and writing and pretty much anywhere where self-confidence would be an asset.

"What gives me the right to be here?" a man recalls asking himself in a more recent 2013 story on imposter syndrome for the American Psychological Association, as he recounted his experience entering a new and challenging work environment. "There's a sense of being thrown into the deep end of a pool and needing to learn to swim. But I wasn't just questioning whether I could survive. In a fundamental way, I was asking, *am I a swimmer?*"

People who experience imposter syndrome are beset with an incongruence of what they can accomplish and what they *think* they can, or should, be able to accomplish. In times of achievement, there is a feeling of phoniness, a constant fear of being "discovered" or "outed" as a fraud, sentiments that perfectly describe the way I often felt at Davidson, both in uniform and in the classroom. I didn't earn high grades; I faked my way to them, constructing papers and writing exams not as displays of what I knew but in hopes of duping my professors into thinking I knew more than I did. When I did get an A on something, I assumed the professor was simply being nice or felt sorry for me. On the court, I played, at root, not to try to win, but to try to fool my teammates and coaches into thinking I was more capable than I felt I was at my core. I had no need to make excuses for my bad games, because poor play was par for my course. Instead, I had to drum up excuses for the games I played well, attributing my best stat lines to the other team taking it easy on me, or the coaches conspiring to get me buckets to deceitfully boost my confidence.

My collapse in the second half of my freshman season at Davidson was, in retrospect, a measure of the exhaustion I felt in trying to keep up this facade, and also a kind of defense mechanism. I would pull myself back on my own rather than risk some massive exposure event.

I vanquished those fraudulent feelings later in my career, notably in Norrkoping and Paks, but the imposter syndrome persisted elsewhere in my life, particularly in relationships, which is why I would often feel compelled to end them at the moment I sensed a woman beginning to really like me. *Her affection is clearly in error*, was my underlying assumption, and even if a woman really was genuine and had legitimate merit in liking me, how dare she like me when I hadn't yet learned to like myself?

Motivated by my failed relationship, I found a new therapist in Pittsburgh, bit down hard, and once again invited everything I could to the surface. I was shocked to discover how much I still had to work through. I looked at old photos of myself and held and loved the person I saw, and I spoke to apparitions of people who'd impacted my life and whose influences I'd yet to move on from. I cried session after session, sometimes not even sure what I was crying about.

"Where do you *feel* it?" my therapist would say, and I'd point to my gut or my heart or my throat.

"Can we stick with that feeling?" she'd say next, and I would nod through my tears and try to breathe into the emotion, working all the while on accepting that not everything needs to be analyzed with words. I worked on accepting a new definition of masculinity, and worked, too, on accepting that being human isn't always a progressive series of jumps from a lesser lilypad to a greater one, but that *stillness* and *peace* and *compassion* are perhaps more noble pursuits.

I also finally found an answer to *Who am I?* The answer is, simply, *Who I am*. I am dynamic and unstable, constantly evolving and shifting. By the time I stop and think about the question, the answer isn't true anymore.

In later sessions I stopped considering my obsessive-compulsive symptoms a "disorder," instead referring to my pattern of thoughts as an obsessive-compulsive *mindset*. My tendency to obsess and be compulsive was and is a real part of who I am, and I felt no need to connotate it negatively. I might never be totally at peace, but I can be at peace with who I am, is what I told myself. In the end then, I did end up killing myself, but only to find myself anew.

In January 2014, after going almost a year without touching a ball or even watching a game, I started working basketball clinics with a Pittsburgh-based organization called The Scoring Factory. The day of my first clinic I arrived at the gym early and changed into basketball sneakers, arranging my laces and socks just so. I walked over to the ball rack and fingered the basketballs as if squeezing prized fruit at the grocery store. Selecting one, I went through the same warmup I'd conducted as a player, even though I wouldn't be playing. Kids a third my age were busy doing much of the same.

A little ways into the clinic I was tasked with explaining a drill to the players, and as I did, I studied their faces for clues, wondering if I sounded like a coach. When I finished the explanation I ordered the players to their respective lines. "Start when you're ready," I bellowed, but nobody moved. A few of the players shuffled uncomfortably and looked at a guy named Pete, who was running the clinic.

"You gotta say 'go', man," Pete told me some seconds later, after he'd barked at the players to begin. When I asked why, he said, "Basketball players are sometimes like trained seals. They need commands." I was floored by this; in a single sentence, Pete had summed up much of my career.

I found a dynamic and nurturing home with The Scoring

Factory and with Pete as a mentor I started teaching others the game. In teaching others the game, I retaught the game to myself, realizing how much I never knew. Somewhere in those first few years I morphed from a player who happens to be coaching to a coach who used to play. Every day, it felt like, I saw in my players reflections of the athlete I largely was during my career: insecure, overly competitive, and unbalanced.

It wasn't just young athletes who fit this description. One evening I sat in on a city-wide meeting of local youth coaches and league administrators and listened as they debated whether or not it was a good idea to mandate the league's players — elementary and middle-schoolers — offer a hand to help up a fallen player on an opposing team. Nearly everyone agreed that it would be sending the wrong message.

Another time, I asked a group of young players what it means to have heart. A boy raised his hand. "It means you don't cry and you don't let anything affect you," he said. "You just play."

My career symbolically looped back around in that moment. Twenty years before, I'd been his age, and just as impressionable. I was now the authority figure, being called to speak. I stared at the kid and thought hard about what to say. It seemed clear that he didn't actually believe what he'd said, but was showing off how tough he was by making a "tough" statement.

We were supposed to be starting practice, but I was unwilling to break the huddle until I properly responded. I asked him, as neutrally as I could, what was wrong with crying. He shuffled his feet and was taken aback. In his head, his statement was unimpeachable. He hadn't been expecting resistance, particularly not from me, another male. He looked around at the other players in the huddle, boys and girls alike, but they were silent.

At the time, my philosophical beliefs about sports were steadily broadening into a kind of cooperative model, in which winning was deemphasized, while my local interests — and instincts — were being employed in helping the group before me realize themselves to the highest degree possible, even if that realization came at the expense of others. My message wasn't quite "win at all costs," but my focus was winning nonetheless, a focus I'm sure my players picked up on. How was I supposed to mold the contrasting beliefs together? How could I tell this kid that it was okay to cry and feel affected by loss and shame while at the same time reinforce the very true message that non-vital emotions often get in the way of success?

I asked the kid if he knew who Michael Jordan was. He did. I instructed him to look up the clip of Michael Jordan crying after winning the 1993 NBA Championship. He said he would. When I finally broke down the huddle and started practice, I thought I'd handled the situation well, by finding an example of perhaps the world's most competitive athlete uncontrollably shedding tears. But then I realized I had copped out. Michael Jordan's tears were only okay after winning, was the indirect message.

The positive transformations in my life haven't come without a fair amount of retroactive introspection — you could call it regret — and I sometimes wonder what it'd be like to go back and redo my career, not with a more athletic body or with different coaches, but with a different mindset. When I think back on my twenty years playing the game, the things that sting the most aren't missed buzzer-beaters or getting dunked on, but rather the ways I didn't always understand what I was doing, the ways I blindly got in line, and the ways I chased the carrot without grasping *why*. Now, as I coach, I often look around at the landscape of youth basketball in America, at the trained seals and vulnerable minds that I'm charged with developing, and ask myself what needs to change. The short answer is, *something*. Here's the long answer:

I once played Monopoly with a friend who, midway through the game, when most of the properties were bought but before any houses or hotels had been erected, suggested we end the game right there, at a time of relative peace and equality. He proposed we co-govern the board, in the process foregoing the greed and debt that would define the evening if we kept on. Nobody would be the mogul of the board, but nobody would be bankrupt, either. It was my friend's turn, and he jiggled the dice as he waited for the rest of us to realize his suggestion wasn't a joke.

We didn't take him up on it, and the game finished, as most do, with one smug winner congratulating himself for his strategizing and three disappointed losers blaming their bad luck. Afterwards, I thought for a long time about my friend's proposal. In a way, he was asking, *Why bother with the toil of competition? Why suffer the angst of potentially losing all you own for a statistically unlikely shot at winning?* The answer to this query, rather obviously, is that we compete because competition is the essence of being human. Sure, losing sucks, but when we do win, it's worth the effort and sacrifice. Passivity makes us dull, while conflict spurns innovation and growth, and the thrill of it all makes us feel alive. We're capitalists, not communists.

Monopoly is just a board game. When somebody wins, the board is cleared and the participants shuffle off to the rest of their lives. The glory of winning and the sting of losing quickly dissolve. Basketball is just a game, too, and in theory should likewise be played with the same contained competitive spirit and perspective as Monopoly. So, if we could all remember that sports are, at root, just games, then all the corruption and abuse that afflict sports would diminish. Right?

This sounds nice, but when we invoke the idea that sports are just games, we forget that sports are, when stripped of their surface layers, a proxy for warfare, mate attraction, and resource secural. We forget that sports are, apart from sex, one of the safest and most publicly sanctioned ways a human being has to unleash his or her primitive instincts, instincts honed over millions of years of fighting to survive in habitats much harsher than an air-conditioned arena. Sports are a way to physically confront our existential insecurities and a way to express violent repressed emotions, like rage and aggression, which would otherwise be illegal to act on. Only through sports can we be so open and honest about our desires to conquer the universe, and each other in the process.

It wasn't always like this. As mentioned, for most of human history, humans played the game of literal survival, fighting nature and each other for supremacy on the Earth, usually as a part of a tribe. When governments grew powerful enough to establish a temporary peace over a large enough area, leaders created games to feed the spirit of survival and war in the people they governed, people whom, for as long as the peace held, no longer needed to fight. The gladiators of ancient Rome are an example of this, as is the aforementioned Mayan game pitz, as is nearly every rivalry in the modern sports landscape.

When the major professional sports leagues were first being established in the early half of the 20th century (baseball in the late 1800s), the United States was either a participant in a major world war or was emerging out of one. This concurrence helped provide perspective, at least for a while. Our heroes were as much the doughboys and GIs who fought and died on foreign soil as they were the athletes who caught balls on domestic manicured outfields. It was okay to metaphorically bleed for the Yankees or the Red Sox, because it was easy to remember that there were American soldiers literally bleeding across both our bordering oceans.

It's no coincidence that the surge of popularity of sports in the United States over the past seventy or so years has coincided with the longest period of relative peace in human history, the post-WWII era. Despite a number of wars and the ongoing threat of terrorism, humans have been safer since 1945 than they've ever been. The proliferation of antibiotics and the evolution of hospital care, among many other developments, have meant that most humans have readier access to life-saving medicine than ever before. The chemical revolutions in agriculture and the boom in global transport infrastructure have meant that greater quantities of food are available to more people. Far too many humans are still unnecessarily homeless, hungry, and sick, but their condition is more a result of inept governing than of resource deficiency or some structural inability to offer help. Today, we've largely conquered nature (although nature is fighting back), and the world's economies are so interwoven that, despite all the international chaos and posturing we read about in headlines, no fair-minded leader really wants to see World

War III.

To state the point again, it's no coincidence that the popularity of sports has risen in proportion to life expectancy. Surviving is much easier now than it was a century ago, but our survival instincts are still very much a part of our genetic expression. If most of us are no longer fighting as hard to survive, then it follows that we could use an outlet for our still-active survival instincts, a way to express our suppressed primitive urges to compete with others. Sports are that release.

In theory, sports are an ideal outlet for both athletes and spectators. The athlete is allowed to tap into his primitive instincts in order to vanquish an opponent, but there are rules of engagement to encourage fair play and there are doctors on standby in case something serious happens. Bumps and bruises are common, but rarely does an athlete die on the field. The average fan, if he's too scared or doesn't have the opportunity to play himself, can hang up a pennant and outsource his instincts to a professional team. It might be nerve-wracking to watch a game, but fans of sports don't often die, either.

Recognizing athletic competition as a modern outlet for primitive instincts is just one interpretation of sports, among many. The modern sporting landscape is complicated, to say the least, but it seems certain we've lost a lot of the perspective with which sports were born, assuming sports ever had it.

On its best days, today's youth sporting landscape is a positive environment where athletes learn to compete, hopefully have fun doing so, and perhaps secure opportunities they might not otherwise have had. On its bad days, today's sporting landscape is a system that shovels as many players as possible into the fire, a system that convinces parents of the need to invest tremendous time, money, and energy into their children's sporting careers, and a system that teaches athletes of all ages that they need to win and be the best in order to feel validated as a human being. It's a system that *suppresses*, rather than expresses, children's joyful competitive spirits.

On its very worst days, and there are a lot of worst days, today's sporting landscape is an abusive system that largely exploits players without empowering them with a corresponding degree of healthy self-awareness and decision-making. It's a system that channels the sporting ethos of ancient times and prepares kids for war, without ever helping them understand what they're fighting for. It's a myth-building system that more or less hijacks young lives, turns human beings into robots, and then spits all but a tiny fraction of those players back out at eighteen or twenty-two into an alien world that they're nowhere near ready to live in. An athlete leaving the game thinks: *I was created by an athletic system that can barely keep up with its own capitalistic endeavors, let alone find ways to both properly develop and take care of its athletes outside the construct of competition. I'm not making anyone any money anymore, and have no more to spend. Away from my sport, I have no idea where I belong, don't know who I am, and don't know how to help myself. I'm fucked, aren't I?*

There are, in my opinion, only two ways that the current culture of sports will shift to a healthier place. The first is if the world goes to war again, in which case we'll be reminded firsthand that sports are a very different kind of game than the one played on the battlefield. In other words, we'll regain some perspective. We get glimpses of what this shift would be like in the aftermaths of national tragedies, like 9/11 and mass shootings, when sporting events are often cancelled or draped in respect for victims. We're reminded of the inherent insignificance of sports. A war would have to affect a critical mass of Americans for this to happen, a critical mass that smaller wars like the ongoing conflicts in Iraq and Afghanistan fail to meet, however horrific their existence.

The second way to positively overhaul sports is if we begin to coach our children differently, by placing an emphasis on cooperation, not competition, and on joy, not anger. Joy cannot be seen as merely the byproduct of a major victory, but as the output that stems from immersing oneself fully into the flow of a game. Similarly, cooperation can't be seen as merely the means by which one team defeats another. It's not a weapon, in other words. Cooperation should be seen, rather, as the way ten players compete in harmonious conflict on a basketball court, even if five players wear red jerseys and the other five wear blue.

Sports don't need to go away, but the narrative that currently surrounds them does, namely, the glorification of competitiveness. The ability to compete was once a vital means of survival for the human race. It's gotten us this far, and it's understandable that we revere athletes who take their crafts very seriously. In a way, those athletes are taking their *survival* seriously, and we, as fans like to live vicariously. But on a finite planet with 7.5 billion people and counting, competition, if it remains a human being's primary drive, will ultimately choke the human race into extinction. As silly or corny as it sounds, equal room, it not more room, must be made in our hearts for cooperation.

To change the way our children think about sports, it seems we'd have to train our children to operate against their natural human instincts, and in order for us as adults to be the teachers they need, we'd have to teach against our own natural instincts, as well. Survival instincts (competition) are hardwired into our genes, and no number of pregame pep talks about being a good sport is going to change that overnight. But again, the goal wouldn't be to erase our competitive natures, but rather to reinterpret them philosophically and to apply them differently. We can begin this effort by tweaking the infrastructure of youth sports on a mass scale. Nobody would tell a child not to run as fast as he can or not to compete to the best of his ability. But we would reframe so much more.

My first suggestion is to eliminate score keeping and stat keeping in every youth basketball league in America, until, say, the 6th grade. Games would be played, but the scoreboard would be kept off. Ideally, the primary emphasis in a no-score, no-stats league would be on the experience of playing, with an equal emphasis on skill development. Imagine the freedom players would have to immerse themselves in the flow of the game, unshackled from the pressures of proving themselves via stats and wins before they're ready, before they even know *who*, exactly, would be doing the proving. Imagine the freedom coaches would have to teach the game, unbounded by the immediate pressures of winning. Youth leagues could also mandate that their players play on different teams each week, so that nobody gets too attached to the idea of "us" vs. "them" too early.

When players get old enough, the scoreboard would be switched on. Two or three years later, in eighth or ninth grade, players would be allowed to enter into more traditional competitive structures, like AAU, and would be allowed to start playing on more permanent teams.

The hope of these changes would be this: even as children get older and more competitive, the lessons of their formative years will help players keep the game, and their place in it, in perspective. Ideally, more children will grow up to see the world less as a place to be conquered at all costs, and more as a single, fragile unit in which mass cooperation is vitally necessary. We don't have the luxury of taking the planet for granted anymore.

My second suggestion, which goes hand in hand with the first, is to develop better mental health training manuals for youth coaches. Instead of overemphasizing future success, we can encourage kids to play *in the moment*, which is the best way to prepare for the future anyway. Three out of four U.S. households with school-age children have at least one child participating in youth sports. That's tens of millions of kids learning from the examples and rhetoric of their coaches. We all share the same future.

Epilogue

Basketball was an exhibition sport at the Olympics as early as the St. Louis, Missouri games in 1904, but it wasn't until 1936, in Berlin, Germany that it became an official Olympic event. Twenty-one teams from the far corners of the world, including Chile, the Philippines, and Egypt, rode steamers across oceans and trains across deserts to Berlin, making basketball the largest team sport at the '36 Games.

Before the tournament began, the Uruguayan delegation, upon seeing the size of many of their opponents, tried to enact a rule prohibiting players over 5'8" from participating. The request was made partially in jest, but it was far from the only oddity that unfolded during the games. The balls, for instance, were visibly lopsided, had bulging laces that interfered with dribbling, and were made from slippery ungrained leather, manufactured by a German company that apparently knew little about basketballs. The games themselves were played outdoors on tennis courts, subjecting players to wind, rain, and sun.

Dr. Naismith was in attendance for much of the tournament, although it took some effort to get him to Berlin. Despite the surge in popularity of the sport he invented, Naismith had been struggling financially for some years, and it was only after a number of charity games were played in the United States, with the proceeds paying for his ticket, that he was able to make the trip to Europe.

While in Germany, Naismith was granted celebrity status and feted everywhere he went, including a dinner attended by Adolf Hitler, with whom he had a brief conversation.

On August 14th, 1936, the American team beat Canada on a muddy court in a torrential downpour by a final score of 19-8, the first of seven straight gold medals for the United States. (Despite the height deficit, Uruguay made it as far as the quarterfinals before losing to Canada.) The *New York Times* article reporting the U.S. victory the next day ran under the headline "SPORT NOW WORLD GAME." Indeed, after the games, the various national contingents, many having seen and played against each other in person for the first time, returned to their respective home countries with new ideas on basketball style and strategy.

Throughout the Olympics, the American team wore white shoes with a red and blue trim, provided for them by Charles Hollis Taylor, better known as "Chuck" Taylor. Taylor, originally from Indiana, had until the early 1930s worked for Marquis Converse, a Massachusetts businessman whose enterprise, the Converse Rubber Shoe Company, originally specialized in making rubber galoshes. In the 1910s, however, Converse, looking to keep his skilled galosh-making workforce employed year round, decided to invest in a new, Oxford-type, non-skid shoe. The new shoe wasn't intended for athletes, but it was nonetheless quickly associated with basketball. Recognizing the potential opportunity for high sales, Converse hired Taylor, a former two-time All-State high school guard in Indiana, to promote and sell the shoe. Taylor and his team, the Converse All-Stars, spent years barnstorming the United States, giving free clinics and spreading both the Converse brand and the game of basketball.

Marquis Converse died in 1931, and Taylor, looking to boost flagging sales during the Great Depression, decided to rebrand Converse's shoe the Chuck Taylor All-Star. He was successful enough to get a deal with USA Basketball, and the 1936 Olympics saw his shoes worn in competition for the first time. Billions of pairs have since been sold, and sales are still strong today, making Chuck Taylors one of the most iconic sneakers of all time.

After the Olympics, Taylor became friends with John B. McClendon, who in 1944 became the head coach at the North Carolina College for Negroes (now North Carolina Central), whose all-African American squad walloped an all-white Duke University team in the first integrated collegiate game in the South.

McClendon is one of basketball's most underappreciated figures. He learned the game from Naismith as a student at Kansas, but, being African-American, wasn't allowed to play on the team itself. (McClendon nonetheless became the first African-American to earn a physical education degree from Kansas). He found his niche as a coach, and won multiple CIAA and NAIA collegiate titles before brief stints as a professional coach with the Cleveland Pipers of the American Basketball League and the Denver Rockets of the ABA (now the Denver Nuggets). McClendon was instrumental in speeding up the pace of the game, and is credited with developing the fast break and the full court press. He also pioneered the "four corners" offense, later made famous by Dean Smith at North Carolina. Julius Erving, the NBA legend, called McClendon the "father of black basketball."

In the 1960s, when Chuck Taylor retired as head promoter and salesman at Converse, he asked his friend

McClendon to take over. McClendon agreed, and spent the next two decades working tirelessly on the behalf of Converse, traveling to fifty-eight countries and delivering countless speeches and free clinics. He worked for a shoe company, but his soul was with the game, and over the ensuing years many international coaches would testify that they learned basketball from McClendon.

By the time the 1992 Olympic games in Barcelona, Spain began, Chuck Taylor was dead and John McClendon was an old man, but the game they helped create, both on the court and off, was on full display. Every single U.S. player had a shoe deal, including Magic Johnson and Larry Bird with Converse, and teams from around the world were displaying the skills they'd picked up from McClendon's clinics. The '92 Olympics also marked the moment when the U.S. team, the original Dream Team, opted against tradition and decided not to sleep in the Olympic Village. Instead, they took over the Ambassador Hotel in a more chic part of town, sparking a new custom that continued through the Rio, Brazil Olympics in 2016, when Team USA stayed on a cruise ship docked at the Pier Maua in Guanabara Bay, a good hour and a half from the athletic venues. The ship featured around-the-clock security, including two hundred and fifty fully-armed soldiers, a bulletproof wall, and Brazilian naval vessels patrolling the surrounding waters. Inside, it was all the pampered luxury you'd expect in a five hundred and fourteen foot aquatic hotel meant to keep twenty-four of the world's best basketball players happy and comfortable. I know, as I was there.

Odds are against me being one the world's twenty-four best players, but in August of that year I flew down to Rio to stay on the ship with a friend who worked for Team

USA. The cruise ship was called *Silver Cloud*, which I thought was perhaps the most ominous possible name for a team with no expectation other than gold. The last time Team USA stayed on a cruise ship, in Athens in 2004, they settled for bronze in perhaps the most disappointing international performance in USA basketball history, vying for the low bar only with their 6th place finish at the World Championships in Indianapolis in 2002.

After one of Team USA's practices I had the chance to speak with Carmelo Anthony, who I hadn't seen in almost a decade. We'd both changed a lot — Carmelo was by then a nine-time NBA All-Star and a four-time Olympian — but then again maybe we hadn't. I felt around him in Rio a lot like I'd felt around him at Oak Hill, a little unsure of myself and eager to find common ground. We reminisced for a few minutes about high school, then I wished him good luck and said goodbye.

On August 21st, 2016, Kevin Durant scored 24 of his 30 points before halftime in leading Team USA to a 96-66 thrubbing of Serbia in the gold medal game. At some point during the first half, as I sat with other Americans in the Carioca Arena 1, I had a startling realization: I loved basketball. It was the strangest feeling, if only that it made me realize I'd never truly loved basketball before, at least not as an adult.

If I could go back in time and attend any sporting event in the history of the world, I would probably choose to travel to the western front of World War I on December 25th, 1914, the site of an impromptu soccer game between Allied and German soldiers.

The soccer game was part of a widespread but unofficial

"Christmas Truce" between the warring sides. Tens of thousands of soldiers participated in the truce up and down the trenches, and there are hundreds of versions of how the truce began, but a classic version goes like this: On Christmas Eve, French and British soldiers heard their German counterparts across No Man's Land singing carols. Surprised, they sung a few carols back. At dawn on Christmas Day, a small party of German soldiers climbed out of their trench and began working their way through the barbed wire and decomposing bodies and artillery craters that defined No Man's Land. The Allied soldiers were initially suspicious, but, seeing that the German soldiers were unarmed, eventually climbed out too. Pleasantries were exchanged, and soldiers from both sides took advantage of the ceasefire to clear the field of dead bodies. The soldiers commiserated about the awful living conditions inside the trenches and discussed which of the type of bullets one least wanted to be shot with. The English gave the Germans boxes of plum pudding, and the Germans gave the English cartons of cigarettes, and, in at least one documented case, a soccer ball was found and a pick-up game organized.

Imagine the purity of such a game, a game played for the sake of the game, for the sake of competition. In the midst of a horrible war, having just dug the graves of their comrades, one imagines that the soldiers felt no need to be nitpicky about a handball. Having spent the previous months firing bullets into flesh, one imagines that neither side was all that upset when they lost.

At the end of the day the soccer ball was put away and the soldiers climbed back into their trenches to resume the war, but, having seen the humanity in their counterparts across the field, refused to fight. Eventually, the frustrated generals behind the lines had to relieve the entrenched soldiers and bring in fresh troops, troops who still largely thought of the enemy as nonhuman.

In June 2016, almost three years after moving to Pittsburgh and just a couple months shy of my trip to the Olympics, I drove to Davidson for my graduating class' ten-year reunion. Several of my former teammates were there, and that Saturday morning we gathered at Davidson's practice facility to play pick-up. After several years of forced indifference to my former college, I'd grown to revere both Davidson and Davidson basketball, and stepping onto the court with my former teammates that day was as meaningful a moment as any I'd been a part of throughout my career. We warmed up and chose teams, and then the ball was checked up to start the game.

It was the first time I'd played against real competition in years. I couldn't run as fast or jump as high as I once could, but I felt joyful and spontaneous and in rhythm nonetheless. In other words, I felt like myself. Even when some of the guys started to trickle off, when 5-on-5 became 3-on-3, I kept pushing us to run it back just one more time, as the thought of having to stop was almost painful. Having finally found a joyful peace with the game, I didn't want to give it up. *This*, I thought, is how sports should be played. Short of taking part of an impromptu pick-up game in the midst of a global war, *this* was as close to a purity with sports as I would probably ever feel.

I've thought often about both the Christmas Truce and that morning playing pick-up at Davidson, and eventually I realized that the real challenge of retiring isn't the cessation of playing sports, it's that you've lost the best way you knew to lose yourself. Committed athletes often comment about how at home they feel on the court, how much like *themselves* they feel when they have a ball in their hands and are scoring at will. I've occasionally thought the same. This is, however, false. In truth, highly successful athletes are *least* like themselves on the court, because to truly play the game you have to let go, and letting go in this respect includes letting go of identity and autonomy.

Dividing a game into two teams and ten players is a convenient and fun way for a fan to watch. It's easy to point to a name on the back of a jersey and say that this or that particular player just scored. But, in the flow of the game itself, the player is identity-less apart from the game, as the best players operate thoughtlessly and instinctually.

In other words, to truly play the game, you have to *become* the game. Becoming the game means playing in the now, and in the now there's no room for the past or future, which are the domains of ego and anxiety. It may sound like I'm speaking in metaphysical hues, but I imagine any athlete who's ever felt "lost" in a game knows exactly what I mean.

When we truly play, we find ourselves by losing ourselves. Retiring, then, means giving up the ability to get lost, and that's what's so difficult for so many athletes. It's a lot like a drug addict trying to get clean. The addict used the drug because the drug helped him forget who he was, and he misses the drug because he doesn't know how to live with himself without it. We find out who we truly are only when we sit still, and a lot of us don't like what we encounter when we don't have distractions handy, no matter how meaningful or important those distractions might be.

I love basketball. I can say that now unconditionally and

without amendment because I once hated the game, and I can say it, too, because I am learning to love *myself* unconditionally and without amendment. I didn't hate the game, I've realized, as much as I hated myself within the game, and my search for peace with the game was really a search for peace with myself.

The most important thing I did when I retired was find the courage to sit still, and the second most courageous thing I did was not turn my back on what came up when I did. In learning to sit still, I died the athlete's death, and have since, through much toil and surrender, been resurrected anew. Not in any religious way, but as a human being exercising my right to keep trying.

Acknowledgments

More gratitude than I know how to convey goes to Brock Green, Mike Ely and Eric Wilson, for showing me how it can be done, to the teammates I'm fortunate enough to call brothers and whose stories I tell with my own, to Coach Steve Smith and Lisa Smith for their sanity and warmth, to Davidson College for being the incomparable Davidson College, to Cole Barton for leading me out of a tough time, to Coach Bob McKillop for never ceasing to try and get the best out of me, to Wahoe India for the experience of a lifetime, to D-Web and SH for for your patient ears and so much more, to my mother for feeding me words, to my father for the work ethic and resiliency, to my sisters for "getting" me, to Mike Main for being the greatest agent ever, to Pete Strobl for giving me a path forward, to Jordan Harbison, Rob Southall, Milan Smiljanic and The Scoring Factory for the camaraderie and the chance to teach, to my wonderful group of players for the chance to learn, to my PGH families for friendship and for keeping me fed(!), to Faith and Alex for the care and love, to Ed and the Lettieris for their constant kindness, to Jeff Schneekloth for the brotherhood, likewise to John and Dom, to Becky Bonner for reading with compassion and for being the perfect friend at the right time, to Maryanne O'Hara for the timely tutorial, to Jocelyn Horner for the blunt appraisals and feedback, to Mary Sico for suffering through early chapters, to my unflinchingly positive and patient editor Michael Shields for giving me a chance, to Chris Thompson and the rest of the team (Richard Roundy, Douglas Grant, Maggie Sachson, Sam Ensogna, Taylor Burnfield, and William Shields) at ATM Publishing for all the effort to make this thing a reality, and, finally, to CGM.

About the Author

Ian Johnson played Division I basketball at Davidson College before playing five professional seasons in European leagues. He coaches basketball in Pittsburgh, Pennsylvania. This is his first book.

41675628R00130

Made in the USA
Middletown, DE
08 April 2019